Stevens Sheppard

I am the King

Being the account of some happenings in the life of Godfrey de Bersac

Stevens Sheppard

I am the King
Being the account of some happenings in the life of Godfrey de Bersac

ISBN/EAN: 9783743413443

Manufactured in Europe, USA, Canada, Australia, Japa

Cover: Foto ©ninafisch / pixelio.de

Manufactured and distributed by brebook publishing software (www.brebook.com)

Stevens Sheppard

I am the King

I AM THE KING

*Being the Account of Some Happenings
in the Life of Godfrey de Bersac
Crusader-Knight*

BY

SHEPPARD STEVENS

BOSTON
LITTLE, BROWN, AND COMPANY
1898

Copyright, 1898,
BY LITTLE, BROWN, AND COMPANY.

All rights reserved.

𝔘𝔫𝔦𝔳𝔢𝔯𝔰𝔦𝔱𝔶 𝔓𝔯𝔢𝔰𝔰:
JOHN WILSON AND SON, CAMBRIDGE, U.S.A.

TO
My Father and Mother

THIS LITTLE BOOK IS LOVINGLY INSCRIBED, WITH
GRATEFUL APPRECIATION OF THEIR
UNWAVERING FAITH.

CONTENTS

Chapter		Page
I	Marian's Tale	1
II	Godfrey's Tale	43
III	Anselm's Tale	151

I AM THE KING

I

MARIAN'S TALE

METHINKS it began that day when my Lady Joscelyn and I shelled peas in the garden, though it were not till many a day later that trouble befel; yet, withal, my mind doth hie back to that hour as it were the beginning of the story. Thou art amazed, I trow, at thought of her ladyship bemeaning herself to such service; but it were not then as now, and many is the day that she hath wrought by my side as she were the wench of some villain and not the child of a knight of renown. Beshrew me! if Friday oft last not from Kalends to Nones, and thence to Ides, and back again to Kalends at Weregrave Manor, and that without meat of fish to help our spare living, and hardly was there a yeoman or churl in Merry England but fared more sumptuously than my master.

But, as I did say before, we shelled peas in the garden that day; rather I did shell the peas, while my lady sat upon the grass, burying deep her hands under the round green kernels, and bringing them slowly to sight again as they were two white flowers in spring pushing through the green sod.

"Marian," quoth she, and she shook the last green globe from her hands, "methinks I grow idle even as I am discontent. Reach hither the basin that I may do my share of the task."

"Nay, nay," I coaxed, for that I would rather see her at play than at work. "The task is but a feather weight. Let Marian do it while thou dost rest;" but she would not, and I needs must push the basin to her hand and see her begin in right good earnest to rattle the peas from the cod.

"An I hearkened to thee, Marian, I would sit ever idle while thou didst toil both day and night. Thou dost now, the work of a man 'twixt dawn and dark, and it were not meet that I should abide in slothfulness and leave my task on thee, thou faithful wench."

I did hold my speech and answer naught, for it was a theme which we oft discussed, but never to agreement; and so peace fell betwixt us, until, breaking open a cod, my lady held it forth to me, saying, "See, Marian, it were small dwelling for so large a family," and would straightway have ripped the peas from the hull an I had not fast held her hand.

"Stay, stay," quoth I. "God's mercy, child! wouldst thou spoil thy fortune thus?"

Marian's Tale

"How now, Marian, what mean you," saith she in surprise; and she did gaze at me for the world like some startled wood deer, save that her eyes were blue with that deep color of cloudless sky on summer day.

"There be nine peas in the cod," saith I, counting them over; "wot ye not that it is a divination cod, and will e'en tell who thy lord shall be?"

"Thou foolish wench, thou art as full of tales and incantations as any old wife," and she made as if to strip the peas from the cod; but I did stay her hand the while I begged her heed me. "If thou didst know how oft my dreams and divinations come to truthful issue thou'st hearken to me. But place the cod over yonder postern and it be sure as sure that he who first steps under will be thy lord."

Her red lips parted over her teeth in a smile which belike seemeth to me to have more of witchery in it than the smile of any creature that e'er lived. "Then, Marian, thy mistress is like to mate with the varlet Giles, who is stable boy, swineherd and kitchen scullion in one, since he most like is to come through the postern first; but if thou wilt so have it, place the cod over the lintel and pray you it so hap there come a worthier knight than Giles Hardpate."

"Heaven forefend, my lady;" and I did try to frown upon her lightness, but rain were as like to come from a cloudless sky as frowns to stay before her teasing face. "This thou must do for thy self, howbeit; should Marian place it for thee, mayhap the charm would fail to work."

"I do but please thee with this mummery," saith she, an she stepped on a loose stone in the wall and placed the cod fairly over the middle of the postern; and yet methinks my lady was monstrous willing for the nonce to please poor Marian. It doth live in my eye still how she looked on that instant as she stood, poised like a bird on a bough, her tiny foot thrust 'twixt the crumbling masonry. She had thrown aside her couvrechief, and her head was bare save for the tressor of ribbon about it. Her hair was as the golden collar and spurs which my master kept in the hutch in his chamber, — save when he did on occasion fare forth arrayed as became his state if not his purse; her skin was like naught so much as the white stream that twice a day I coax from Malkin's soft dugs; and the witchery of her smile, now tender, now teasing, nor heaven nor earth owns aught to which it can be likened.

She was apparelled that day — how well do I remember — in a cote of white, all covered, save the long close-fitting sleeve, by her surcote of dull green wool. Around the neck — below her white camisa — and about the foot was wrought a narrow band of stitchery in divers colors. Despite that we did weave the cloth of her surcote ourselves and dye it; it was fair to look on, and I thought no damsel of the court could be more quaintly bedight.

My Lady Joscelyn had scarce seated her and turned again to the task ere a blast from a bugle told of a visitor at the Manor portals. Such a sound was used to bring my lady to a sore pitch of curiosity withal, and send her right swiftly to the nearest lattice; but this day she paid no heed to it till I spake thereon, wondering who stood without.

"'T is but my cousin de Hardecute; I know his blast right well," saith she.

"And dost thou not go to meet him, my lady?" quoth I.

"Nay, I go not. I am aweary, and my father will do the honors of the Manor," saith she with petulance. And then I saw that which oft before had thrust itself upon me; despite that her father did show the knight, Hugh de Hardecute, much favor, my lady ill brooked his presence at Weregrave, and misliked the gallant himself right heartily.

Our task was near wrought, when, on a sudden, the postern door fell apart, and under the very spot where my lady's cod lay stood her kinsman, still clad in his riding cape, the dust of travel unwashed from his person. He wore beneath his cape a short tunic of rich purple girt with a jewelled belt, from which depended a basclard;[1] his shoes were pointed, as the style demanded, and richly wrought with threads of gold and color; from under his flat cap of purple his hair fell in curls the which would well have graced a damsel's head.

My lady went white with fear an she saw him, for that he stood beneath her cod the charm foretold him her lord.

Looking on him I did bethink it passing strange that a damsel should so blench from the thought of calling him lord, for he was lusty and fair to look on, e'en though his manner of moving bespoke him something slothful, and his girth unfolded a tale of indulgence at table. He stood in the door and gazed on my lady a time ere he spoke, and rancor made deep furrows in his forehead.

"How now, fair cousin; methinks the hospitality of Weregrave hath suffered a falling off from other days, that thou dost leave thy guest and kinsman to seek the mistress at her tasks," quoth he.

"Mayhap thou dost forget that in other days the chatelaine of Weregrave had not to play the kitchen wench as well;" then saith she, "Thou art welcome, though tardily met," and she gave him her hand, which, as he bent to kiss, I did see the color flame in her cheek, for that her conscience told her she had done amiss; nathless she held her little pate as high

[1] A long dagger.

as she had the right on it. I doubt not from the countenance of Sir Hugh that he did fairly understand my lady's mood, for he frowned yet the more.

"By my faith," quoth he, "a right fitting sport is this for one of thy degree. I pray you have done with it and walk a space with me, for I would have a word with thee."

"Nay, good cousin, sport it is not, I do beseech thee know, but right dire necessity that doth tie me to my labors, which an it please you, I leave not till they be done."

At this his brow grew more black, and I did catch a gleam within his eye which gave me to doubt that it was accident withal that caused his careless foot to overturn our basin heaped with shelled peas, — which it so happed was the greater part of our dinner, I meaning to make them into a savory pottage before the hour of tierce.

My lady was to her feet on the instant, and a frown a'most as dark as his, ruffled her pretty brow.

"How now, Sir Awkward, seest thou the hurt thy careless foot hath wrought? Stay, Marian," saith she, as I did go upon my knees to gather up the peas, "Sir Hugh will mend his fault by himself restoring them to the basin."

"Now, by the bones of St. Christopher, that will I *not*," saith he in tones of choler.

"Now, by thine own bones, which thou 'lt

bend to do the deed, thou wilt," quoth my lady in tones so soft atop, so cold beneath; and these two did face each the other with crest uplifted, for all the world as two young cocks o' the yard measure strength ere they give battle.

It was my lady's eye that flinched not, my lady's head that kept aloft, and it were Sir Hugh that mumbled somewhat about "An it please you, fair cousin — " as he got him to his knee and shovelled the peas in the basin with such ill haste that sticks and pebbles made quite half, and I was a good hour by the dial getting them clean, and tierce was come ere the pottage had begun a-boiling.

When Sir Hugh had made an end of his task and was come to his feet again, he did hastily leave my lady and go to the Manor, and right sore displeased was he in going, I trow.

The postern had scarce fallen together behind him ere my lady sprung upon the broken wall and swept the peas cod from the lintel.

"A pox on thy silly superstition, Marian; see what thy fooling hath wrought," saith she, and I saw she was sore vexed with me, with herself, with her kinsman, and belike even with the harmless cod, which she ruthlessly crushed neath her tiny buskin.

"Beshrew me, my lady, but thou art ill to please, an a knight who hath both gold and lusty looks satisfy thee not," quoth I.

"By my halidom," swore she, for my lady did on occasion use a right round oath, "an I go unmated to my grave, I wed not with Hugh de Hardecute. Dost think I care aught for thy silly superstition to believe that I am fated by yonder green cod to wed a man I hate? Nay, e'en if such fate did bind me I would crush it as I do this," and she ground the cod in the dirt till it were but a green stain on the path. Hardly had I seen her in so great a rage since we were children and she did blow her brief passion out on aught that did offend her.

I wisely held my peace, and but that I could not refrain my head from wagging she had not known my thought.

"Nay, nay, Marian," her voice fell a-pleading, and all her fire died on the instant, "nay, thou dost not believe this foolish tale, thou canst not; nathless, I would be right glad an Hugh were but one step closer kin, for that then he would be within the degree forbidden," and saying this she flung herself beside me and hid her face for tears; and thus I could see that despite her pretty defiance she did half believe and wholly fear.

"There my dove, there my pretty one, weep no more I do beseech thee, else will thy Marian's heart break o' sorrow. The cod hath lied and thou'lt wed as it please thee," saith I,—which God pardon, for I believed it not, but

I would ha' forsworn my name an it suffice to stay my lady's tears.

When she had made an end of crying I begged her tell me why she so misliked her cousin Hugh. "For," saith I, "he is comely to look on and of goodly size."

"He hath stature, Marian, but lacketh strength. I do like a man who hath muscles like tempered steel," she did object.

"His hair," saith I, in continuance, "is fair and fine, a'most as bright as thine own."

"The color which best pleaseth me is brown of a somewhat dark shade," quoth she.

"His eyes — thou 'lt agree he hath good gray eyes?" But no she would not.

"Say rather green, Marian, save when anger doth turn them black. Didst see how they flashed when I defied him leave the peas where his churlish foot had put them? Beside, an they please me, his eyes should be blue, — as blue as speedwell flowers new opened."

"His cheek — thou canst not in reason deny his cheek is fair and smooth."

"An it please you I grant his cheek is smooth; but I like not smooth cheeks. Methinks I do even like a little seamed scar beneath the eye," saith she as one who dreamed.

Then quick I turned upon her. "Where hast thou seen him?" quoth I, at which she went as red as the dawn ere yet it deepens into day, and her tongue fell into so mighty a tangle she was not able to give answer withal, to so plain a question. At length she did stammer forth that 't was but a maiden dream.

"Nay, nay, my pretty, that will I not believe. A maiden dream not like is to wear a *little seamed scar* beneath his eye."

At which she went mightily red again.

"Thou art something right in this matter, Marian," saith she with dignity," for I once beheld a youth not unlike to him whom I pictured. Dost thou remember a year agone, when our feudal lord, Roger Fitz Rainfrey, gave his daughter in marriage to the noble knight William de Pretelles, and my father being bidden we journeyed thither? Thou knowest of the feasting, the games and sports, of how the knights gathered to joust against each other in friendly contest. 'T was then I saw this youth who bore himself in so knightly a fashion that he was counted victor o'er and o'er. Mine eyes did fasten upon him, and methinks he pleased me more than any man that ever I beheld. He was not comely, Marian, nay, I think most would name him uncomely; but his uncomeliness pleased me more than fair locks and smooth cheeks. I marked well one damsel who tarried in the household of Roger Fitz Rainfrey, how she watched his every move and hung upon his acts. She sent to him by a page a sleeve of her gown as favor, the which when he took it I saw him kiss ere he fastened on the token; then he made obeisance to that part of the gallery where she sat; but, withal, it seemed to me that there was little of joy in his face at her favor, and I bethought it most unmaidenly for one to gaze thus and show such fancy where it was so little valued. But that concerns me not, Marian, save that I like a modest maid. She sat with the household of our lord in seats of consequence, while I and my father did bide far off in much humbler places. It doth vex me sore when I remember how lack of gold hath so reduced us that we must needs stand little above the yeomanry; and it grieved me yet more to see the poor favor bestowed on my father, who was given a low seat at table, and all but rudely jostled by the serving men. This to a knight whose name once rung through England, because, forsooth, he is now both poor and old. It did make my blood burn, and I was glad to be away, albeit it was my first and last glimpse of the world."

"And this knight, didst hold speech with him?" I questioned.

"Nay, I do not think he even saw me, but I did hear his name, — Godfrey de Bersac; like you it, Marian?"

Now there befell a thing which seemed passing strange, for it were scarce six days — nay, if memory doth not trick me, 't was but a five day after that a strange bugle blast summoned the inmates of Weregrave.

On this time my lady and I passed right quickly to the nearest lattice and gazed forth. There stood without a knight, a squire, and a churl who led a mule well laden with baggage. The apparel of the knight and the rich housing of his horse bespoke him a man of degree. While we gazed, Giles brought word to my master that a knight, one in the service of Roger Fitz Rainfrey, begged admittance and hospitable assistance, seeing that the jennet which the youth rode had cast his left hind shoe.

"Admit them at once," commanded my master, "and send straightway to the forest for Clement, that he may shoe the jennet, if perchance the youth must prick forward on his journey. Come, my daughter, we will to the outer gate to greet our guest."

I watched my master and my lady as they did cross the court and meet the strangers when the great gate was opened. Entered first the knight, clad in a hauberk and chausses of chain-mail, over which he wore a surcote of rich yellow samite, wrought with a powdering of crosses done in fine stitchery of silver. His bonnet was of the same yellow, and concealed a head close cropped, as I did see when he doffed its covering at sight of my lady. His spurs were of gold, as was also his finely wrought collar. For weapon he wore a baselard girt at his belt. His squire was clothed in body armor of quilted stuff, and wore collar and spurs of silver. He wore an anelace[1] at his belt, and carried the knight's helmet and lance with its double-pointed pennon of yellow, bearing three silver crosses.

On the instant that the knight did sight my lady, he got him from his horse and to his knee with such quickness and grace as would commend him to a damsel. When he had made an end of kissing her hand he stood gazing at her as he were a moonstruck villain, and my lady was scarce a whit better, going white and red, and drooping her head as she ne'er did in my knowledge afore; and all unwitting was I of the cause till they entered the hall; then saw I that his hair was of a darkish brown, his eyes like speedwell flowers new opened, and that he bore a *little seamed scar neath the left eye.*

My master spake as they entered; saith he, "By my faith, Sir Knight, that can I not allow, that a wayfarer, and one who rides from London, should pass the gate of Weregrave and not stop the night at smallest. An thy business cry not haste, I beg thee tarry and give us news of the town."

"Gramercy for thy courtesy, worthy sir, which I do accept the more readily that I am

[1] A short dagger.

the bearer of messages to thee from thy lord, Roger Fitz Rainfrey."

"Thou art then doubly welcome; but of thy business hereafter; we will first to thy comfort. What ho, there, Giles, — I say Giles. Come, sirrah, foot it more quickly an thou want not a good basting! Bring hither a bath and prepare a chamber for the travellers. Whilst thou dost refresh thyself and remove the soil of travel, gentle sir, I will to the court and see to the unlading of thy baggage," at which my master hurried forth, and I, awakening to the knowledge that the day was getting forward and the hour of tierce not far distant, did away to the kitchen, though I was sore tried at thought of missing aught that passed 'twixt my mistress and the fair gallant Sir Godfrey.

As I passed to the kitchen I remembered me with joy that there hung upon a hook beside the chimney-place a flitch of bacon — being a most unwonted luxury with which our poor table would be mightily helped this day. Wot ye then my feeling upon entering the door to behold the last of that tasty bit disappear with a gulp down the throat of my master's hound. . . . Seeing me, he made a bolt for safety; but I, seizing a flesh hook, and catching him by the skin of his neck, held on valiantly, and basted him with a right good will, though his strength was no light matter to contend against.

When at length he did twist himself from my grasp, and sped through the door, in my wrath I sent after him an iron pot, the which, God give me pardon, but missed my lady's head by a trifle.

"God's mercy, Marian, hast thou taken leave of thy wit? An the saints had not watched over me I had been fairly sped by thy careless missile," saith my lady, right sorely vexed at poor Marian, at which my feeling burst forth, and I fell a-weeping.

"The fault lieth not with Marian, my lady, but with my master, thy father, who hath forbade me set the nightly bowl of curds and cream for Robin Goodfellow, which thou well knowest so angers the sprite that naught but ill hath befallen this three day. Malkin did overturn the basin of milk this morn, the pottage burned to the pot when I did cook the breakfast, and now the hound hath gulped the flitch of bacon, and there be three travellers within our doors and naught wherewith to feed them. All this I did foresee when I sneezed after I was out of my pallet, and I was for going back to break the charm, but that I heard my master's voice in a right lusty roar, and dared not stop," saith I 'twixt sobs I could not stay.

"Thou canst not mean, Marian, that the hound hath devoured all the meat! Bethink you, there is surely something?" saith my lady, so mightily disturbed that for the nonce she thought not to chide me for my superstition, which she ever called silly and unchristian.

"Nay, but I say truth, my lady; the hound hath devoured all, and there be naught to set before thy noble guests save cheese and bread and butter, with some onions from the garden, and a pottage of peas. Not a stoup of wine, or a flagon of ale to wet such poor fare withal; naught save our own home-brewed mead."

"And this young gallant of the court, Marian, he will think thy master no better than a villain, since he doth fare as they," saith she, mightily disturbed. "Thou must do something, — thou must. Hark ye, Giles shall to the river and catch a fish, which, being Friday, will serve the occasion."

'T was vain that I did remind her that Giles was but an indifferent fisherman, and the fish wary as well as scarce — seeing we had so oft tried thus to fill our empty paunches. "Giles must, and he *must*," quoth she. "And as thou lovest me, Marian, set forth somewhat at the hour of tierce that shall not bring me to blush. Dress the fish as only thou canst, and serve it forth with a sauce colored with saffron and flavored with herbs and spices;" so saying, she departed the kitchen, and left me to my well-nigh hopeless task, the first step of which being to lay hands on that villain Giles and bid him to his quest.

I lifted up my voice to its fullest compass,

and shouted, "Giles, Giles;" then I did pause for answer, and, none coming, I called once again, "Giles," at the which he roared in mine ear an "Aye" so loud that I was frighted beyond measure and thought the devil was come himself to fetch me. When I saw it to be but Giles, who had crept unawares in my rear, I reached forth and cuffed him with a will.

"Take that, thou malapert knave, for so frightening thy betters," saith I.

"By St. Hilary," quoth he, catching his jaw, "thy hand, Marian, is no whit softer than the heel of my lady's white mule. Beshrew me, but I think thou hast broken my jaw."

"I would I had, for mayhap, then, thou wouldst learn to leave alone the oaths of thy betters and confine thy villain tongue to thine own Saxon saints," saith I, — for it angered me that Giles did ever strive to ape those above him.

"Nay, but my jaw is still strong for many a good round Norman oath, the which I mean to use now by my right, since I am become my master's squire."

Thereupon I set my hands to my waist and laughed as I would die afore I stopped. "Thy master's squire — ha! ha! ha! — thou a squire — ha! ha! ha! This goeth beyond thy wildest wit," saith I, 'twixt bursts of laughter. "Thou varlet, thou hind, thou Saxon swineherd, with no swine to tend, thou 'lt claim knighthood o' thy master next. It will be thus " — and I seized me a flesh whittle from the table near by and struck his shoulder three times with the flat of the blade — "' Rise, Sir Giles de Hardpate;' and," quoth I, "he'll give thee to thy coat of arms a swine's head, a kitchen pot, and a horse bridle, to show how various a knave thou art."

Giles caught the whittle from my hand in hot anger, threatening to spit me thereon, — which I feared not, seeing his rage was ever quick in passing.

"If I be not my master's squire, what other is? When he rides forth, go I not with him, bearing his shield? Doth not a knight's squire thus?" quoth he, with air of triumph. Then suddenly bethinking me what I desired of Giles, I deemed it wiser not to contend further with him, or tell him that which he well knew, namely, because poverty had so reduced my master, nathless, it had not exalted Giles.

"Stand thou no longer prating, boy, but to the river and catch a fish 'gainst thy master's dinner," saith I. "The hound hath gulped the flitch of bacon, and there be not a gobbet[1] for dinner an you bring not back a fish."

"Tell me not, Marian," saith he, laying his hands on his paunch with a look of great dolor, — "tell me not that savory flitch of bacon hath gone to line the inside o' that base-bred

[1] Mouthful.

hound. I have e'en dreamed of it two nights a-running, thinking, in my sleep, that I did taste it."

"And thou shalt nevermore taste it save in dreams; so get you to the river, and on pain of death come not again till thou hast a fish. Get you gone;" and I did try to hustle him out.

"That will I not, wench, for it were but wasted time. I have e'en fished the stream till the few fish remaining, when they but glimpse my leathern jerkin, say, one to the other, here cometh Giles o' the hungry paunch; and they straightway to their hollows, where they warily lie till patience is worn through. They know me like a brother, — an evil brother who would eat them."

"None the less must thou go again; 'tis my lady's wish, and as thou art now a squire of dames thou canst not refuse the command of any damsel of degree," at which saying Giles packed, wearing a grin as broad as his countenance, for that I had so addressed him.

Surely the saints looked with pity on our necessity that day, and so bewildered the wary fish that he failed to recognize Giles, and thus fell a prey to the slyly offered bait: ere he knew his ill fate, he was a-boiling in my trivet, sending forth an odor so savory as to whet appetite to a keen edge.

When all was prepared, the table spread and

seats placed on the daïs for my master, my lady and Sir Godfrey, below for the knight's squire and henchman, and the few ragged retainers who were all that remained of a once goodly company of men-at-arms that were used to follow my master's banner and carouse at his board, I bade Giles summon the company to dinner with a loud blast on the horn, and then to make him ready with jug and basin to act as ewer, the which he did with such awkward and unready hands that he was come nigh to empty the basin in the knight's lap. It occurred on this wise: —

Giles was used to see my master dry his hands upon the napkin; but Sir Godfrey touched not the cloth when it was passed to him, but gently waved his hands in the air — which they do say is the fashion of the court. At the first motion that costrel, Giles, flinched as it were a blow aimed at his worthless pate, and scarce escaped turning the contents of the basin over the youth.

I would I might ha' cuffed him then and there, but was so situate I perforce must wait till later, — when, I do promise, I did it in so hearty a manner that Giles maintained it had rolled up usury faster than a Jew's loan.

But to my tale: my master's first question to his guest was as to what news he brought.

"As to that," saith he, "the town, nay all England, speaks of naught save the Holy Wars, the Crusade upon which Richard so soon sets forward. Minstrels sing of Jerusalem's woes, and the valiant deeds already done for her; they fire youth and age alike with longing to out-match what has been with greater things to be. The greatest names in England have enrolled themselves under the banner of the cross, and, down to the humblest, they flock in thousands to assume the sacred emblem. The Pope hath promised forgiveness of sins to all who go on this Crusade, and there be many who seek thus to rid them of the torment of an evil conscience. Great sums are needed for the war, and the King most readily disburthens all whose money is a burthen to them. It hath been said that one of the courtiers jesting him of this, he made answer, 'I would sell London an I could find a chapman.' The day hath been set for the departure; and upon the octave of the nativity of St. John the Baptist, Richard of England meets Philip of France at Vezelai, and from thence they press forward to Messina."

"Ah," saith my master with a sigh, "would God that age had not so dried the sap in this old frame, and I might buckle on harness and set lance in rest in so holy a cause!" and he tangled his fingers in his white beard as he would pluck it off and be again an unshaven youth.

"I would it were even as thou sayest, for then would the Crusade gain an arm strong for defence and mighty in assault. The fame of Ralph de Ardennes' deeds are still sounded by minstrels as a ensample to younger knights," saith Sir Godfrey, making my master a low salutation; whereupon my lady flashed him a look so grateful as would fair mislead the youth to think it of a warmer hue.

"And I," quoth she, with eyes a-sparkle, — "I would I were a man, as thou so oft hath wished, my father; then would I harness and away, and, by our Ladykin, I would e'en bear myself in such fashion as not to dim the fair glory of thy fame an I could not add lustre thereto."

"Say not thus, fair maiden, I do beseech you, for, by St. Christopher, thine eyes can now inspire greater deeds than ten knights could achieve an they fought every hour for a ten year. This being so thou must surely see thou canst do better service for king and cause as thou art," and he bent upon my lady his gaze, at once so bold and so respectful, that her eye faltered not or fell, and there passed a look betwixt them as their hearts had met and kissed.

My master seemed ill pleased seeing this, and the hound, putting up his nose to beg at this moment, got a smart rap for his pains.

"Let us to our business, gentle sir. Thou didst say, I do bethink me, that thou wert bearer of a message from Roger Fitz Rainfrey.

Prithee acquaint me with its purport," saith he in somewhat sour tone.

"I am sent to thee and my cousin of Hardecute with greetings, to say that by the king's decree[1] all who go not to the Crusades shall pay a tithe of their income of the present year as well as a tithe of their chattels, the following articles excepted therefrom: arms, horses, and garments of men-at-arms. He begs thee and all others who hold knights fees of him to come or do their diligence to send the sum with all possible speed."

My master's face looked monstrous sober at hearing this, and my lady went pale thinking of all it meant; but both were too full of pride to say aught, though it were easy to see that whereas my master's tithe were but a pittance the raising of it would entail much hardship.

"Thou art like to have greater reward for thy pains with our kinsman of Hardecute. His tithe will be unto mine as the fat kine to the lean. Nathless, on thy return I will have the sum in readiness for thee," saith he, with voice which would be light and could not.

"By my faith! my cousin is far too young a knight and a lusty to be content with paying

[1] It was enacted by King Henry at Le Mans that all persons who should not go on this expedition should not only pay the tithe, but no one should swear profanely or play at games of chance or dice; and no one after the ensuing Easter should wear beaver or gris, or sable or scarlet; and that all should content them with two dishes. — ROGER DE HOVENDEN.

tithes in this matter with aught save blows. I return with him and fifty good men-at-arms, or I do hold him no true knight."

At which my lady did quirk her mouth in a little unbelieving turn, as I have ever seen her do when she doubted thy speech. "An thou bring not a bag of gold in the stead of thy kinsman, I ne'er shall prophesy again," quoth she.

"Peace, girl; thou speakest of things beyond thee," saith my master, waxing in wrath as ever when she did flout at Sir Hugh: and Lady Joscelyn kept silent, but with unbelieving look, which spake as plain as words.

'T was here that I did lose run of their speech, though it beseemeth me that the knight spoke out with haste and hotness in his cousin's defence; but I could take no account of such trifle when I beheld the youth recklessly cast his trencher[1] among the rushes to stop the pleading of that greedy hound, — which having it, he sniffed disdainfully withal, seeing it was but flavored with fish, and his inside aready well lined with the purloined flitch o' bacon. I bethought me Giles would ha' had a fit seeing

---

[1] It was the custom at this time to make bread of a secondary quality of flour which loaves were pared and cut in thick slices and were called trenchers because they were to be carved upon. In the household of the wealthy these trenchers were afterwards thrown in a basket and given in alms to the beggars at the gate. Among the poorer people they were eaten after use.

his dinner thus cast away. It was with great trial that I could rouse him to take the jug and basin and again act as ewer ere the guests passed from the table.

The youth tarried with us the night, and on the morrow rode early, my lady and Sir Ralph attending him to the court to bid him farewell till he should come again: after which there followed on this seven days of heaviness for my lady, — days when she forgot to work, sitting with idle hands, and eyes gazing into other worlds, or flying with the speed of a lapwing to the lattice an the least noise stirred in the court.

On the eighth day, saith she to me, with eyes amost o'erflowing, "Marian, I fear me some evil hath befallen the youth, else would he have returned ere this. I sorrow much at thought of this, since the holy wars are thus bereft of a high heart and a strong arm," saith she; and I could but gather her close and fondle the bonny head, and make as if I thought her sorrow all for Jerusalem's loss; and while I held her thus, afar there sounded a bugle blast, and my lady, starting away, wore such a look of radiant joy in her eyes, it fast drank up the water there.

When Sir Godfrey was come, and without Sir Hugh, as she said, my lady could not withhold her quip; quoth she, "And our kinsman of Hardecute, with his fifty men-at-arms? I see them not, unless, perchance, thy squire doth bear them concealed within yon leathern bag, on which he bestows so great care."

Sir Godfrey's brow grew dark. "Thou hast proved true prophet, my lady; I would I could say otherwise. Our cousin is content to fight only with gold in this cause."

Three days did Sir Godfrey tarry this time, — three days, in which he followed my lady's steps, hung on her words, and did woo her in such impassioned, overwhelming manner, yet, withal, so tender, that she must needs have given over her heart to his keeping an he had not already netted it with his loving glances.

Sir Ralph saw naught of what went forward 'neath his eyes, for that the getting of his tithe did greatly trouble him. Thus my lady was left to three days of joy; and when they were sped, and the even of the last was come, a heavy shadow lay on her face at thought of so soon parting from Sir Godfrey.

'T was then that I became unwitting hearer of their converse, it happening thus: —

I sat in the chamber, which was twilight dim, and dozed upon the settle, and dreamed a heavy dream, that my lady stood beside a bier and wept grievously; when, on a sudden, voices did pierce my vision, and opening my eyes I saw my bonny child and her lover near the lattice, where the fading light of day did outline their two dark shadows. My lady's voice spake in tone so pleading soft:

"Must thou indeed ride to-morrow? Tarry yet another day, I beg thee."

"Speak not thus to me, gentle child, for mine own weak heart doth join with thee and make a mighty foe for me to o'ercome. I have lingered now longer than doth become a soldier. Shear me not of my manhood, I do beseech thee."

"That I could not an I would;" and I could see by her lifted head that she was proud in speaking thus. She touched the white cross on his shoulder. "He who bears this can fail in naught," saith she.

"Nay, my love, I beg thee try not to fit a saint's nimbus round thy soldier's head. Zeal for Jerusalem in bondage burns not so great within my heart as hope of fame, though I be fair Christian and true knight. I go forth unknown, to win a name; poor, hoping for fortune and thee: also because Richard, my king, doth lead, and I would follow an he marched heaven or hellward. Canst thou accept so self-seeking a knight, Joscelyn?" and he did hold forth his hands to her; she, placing her own within, saith in tones of love:

"I would not have thee other than thou art, Godfrey. Thy honesty doth cover all fault an there be any; but I do wish" — and I heard her voice falter almost to a sob — "I do wish thou wert but now returned." Then the sob did break forth in right earnest.

He caught her to his heart, and holding her head 'gainst his breast he fondled it with loving hand.

"Sweetheart, sweetheart, grieve not thus at my going," I heard him say. "I will return in safety, I do pledge thee."

"Thou art over-presumptuous in such speaking, beloved. It were not well to tempt the wrath of God thus, — and — and there be other dangers. If, perchance, another fairer than I should catch thine eye, — I am but a country maid, and I forget not the damsel who showed thee such favor at the tourney." At which he fell a-teasing her for sheer fulness of content.

"By my faith, now do I know that thou carest for me, when thou wilt let the shadow of another maid so fret thee." Then seeing my lady ill liked his teasing tone, saith he, straightway growing serious, "Trouble not for my fealty, beloved. Godfrey de Bersac will return as he went, thy loyal knight and servant. And thou, sweet, thou wilt abide my coming and let none steal my treasure?"

"My heart shall wait, beloved, and stand still with longing till thou come again," saith she.

"What means this half pledge, Joscelyn?

Shall another take thee from me?" he did question, a doubt coming in his voice.

"Nay, nay, Godfrey, believe me, nay. I know not what frights me; I only know, like a maid, that I do fear," and I knew that my lamb was thinking on the peascod and that which it had foretold.

'T was then that the villain Giles came a-stumbling at the door, and these two did start asunder in haste, whilst I crept softly in the shadow near the door so that when Giles entered, bearing a light, I seemed to follow him. He fastened the candle to the spike on the chimney-shelf, and I seated me near with my work, — for while the youth abode with us we kept late hours, oft not seeking our beds till a full hour past candle lighting.

Sir Godfrey and my lady talked apart, but not in tone so low but I could catch me most on it an I strained my ears, which I promise you I did. She bade him fetch thither his helmet that she might fasten a favor thereon; and when he was come with it, he held it for her while she did bind over it with a silken cord, a fine mesh net of her own weaving. "The glint of gold which thou seest 'twixt the silk, Godfrey, is a tress of my hair woven in. I pray thee wear my poor gift till thou return," saith she in tone so loving sweet.

"If any rob me of it, beloved, he first must take the head beneath," he did protest.

"God forbid!" exclaimed my lady, reverently crossing herself.

Well, on the morrow he rode at dawn, and my lady watched him over the drawbridge and away, till he was but a speck on the distant road. Ere he went he bent from his horse and took her hand; kissing it, he did gaze within her eyes as one who leaves his soul behind; and I do think that look of love and longing must yet linger in her memory as it doth still in mine.

Thenceforward life at Weregrave was ne'er the same; not that my lady moped, for that she did not, though she sorely missed the youth, and was ever restless at the slightest noise without, — which was passing foolish, seeing he was hardly set forward on his journey, and not like to come again, at soonest, for a two year. But it is aye thus with maids who love; they be ever bereft of reason.

The change of which I speak more rested with my master than my mistress, strength seeming to fall from him each day, and age to come on apace.

It were scarce a month after Sir Godfrey's going that he broached to my lady his wish that she listen to Sir Hugh de Hardecute and wed with him. My lady scarce seemed to give his word serious weight, but saith with a flout, "He needs not a wife, my lord; best send him a distaff and bid him learn true housewifely ways."[1]

At which my master's wrath blazed fiercely. "Peace, girl; am I to be worded by a foolish wench. Give heed to what I tell thee, and cease thy fleering, for thou wilt remember it with sorrow when he is thy lord. I have e'en given thee too great liberty of action and speech."

"I meant not to word thee, father, by my faith, but surely thou knowest I can never wed with my cousin Hugh," saith she, in gentle tone, for she did sorrow at vexing him.

"Wherefore not?" he made demand.

"I love him not," saith she, with hesitation.

"Thou canst do thy duty. That will suffice."

"I would never know happiness thus. Oh, my father, condemn me not to such misery," she fell a-pleading.

"Happiness!" and he did seem to brush it aside as it were a trifle. "Sages say 't is but a trick of the mind. Think thou art happy, and so it is. Joscelyn, hark you, this marriage must be an I would or no. Canst thou not see, girl, that my days grow few, my arm weak? Who will be thy defence when I be gone?

---

[1] Several persons sent a present of a distaff and wool to one another as a significant hint that whosoever declined the campaign would degrade himself as much as if he did the duties of a woman. — GEOFFREY DE VINSAUF.

Thy beauty is a menace to thee, thine obscurity thus far thy safeguard. The times are troublous, and grow more so now that the king is gone. If some licentious noble chance to see thy face and covet thy beauty, what defence can I, a weak old man, give, backed by some half a score of starved retainers? What help would there be for thee, my child?"

"The help of God, which ever stretches forth in the cause of the innocent, my lord," quoth she, solemnly.

"As thou sayest, He may be good knight for a damsel's trust; but, by my halidom, I had rather my good right arm and fifty strong yeomen to fight such battle," he made answer; for, as thou 'lt see, my master was nothing religious. "Thy kinsman is rich; he will surround thee with safety and keep thee in plenty. Then can I go hence in peace, seeing that all is well with thee."

"Say not so, my father, my father. Thou wouldst condemn me to certain misery to escape possible evil. Let me bide unwed, I pray thee."

"I have spoken, girl. A father's right is not to be lightly set at naught.[1] See that thou bend thy will to mine, else will I break it."

"Then must it break, father, for I am not

---

[1] At this time a father had absolute right to give his daughter's hand in marriage, and, should she be orphan, the feudal lord or the king himself claimed this power.

able to bend it," saith she, in sadness, as she did pass from the chamber.

No more was spoken of the hated marriage for many weeks, my lord desiring to give the child occasion to overcome her wilfulness; but my lady read his silence otherwise, so used was she to bend him to her wish. As day sped after day, she regained in part her bright spirit, and 'gan to look to the long distant day of Sir Godfrey's coming. Never, I think, did she confess to her father her love for the youth, knowing well that such secret agreement as rested bewixt them would but anger him the more and hurry forward her sorry fate.

On a sudden the trouble fell as a storm from the heaven where no cloud is. Sir Ralph summoned my lady to his chamber, and long they held speech; so long that I grew full of fear, seeing that I had had of late many ill signs, having spent the night with heavy and awesome dreams, and begun the morn with putting my buskin on the wrong foot, and spilling salt, it falling toward my lady, — the which every one doth know is sign of grievous misfortune.

When she at last came forth the color was fled her bonny face, and the line of her mouth so straight and tight drawn I could not think me it would ever again bend itself to gracious curves of mirth: and it was months, aye, years, ere I once more beheld the Joscelyn of old, and sad and bitter happenings lay between.

Saith I, holding forth my arms to her, "My dove, what ails thee? Tell thy Marian?" but she came not to my breast as her custom was when trouble befell, but smiled a smile, distant far from mirth, and saith, laying her hand in my outstretched one, "Thou art in error, Marian, naught troubles me; I am most happy, since I wed in a month's time. The preparation goeth on without delay. My father hath aready sent to the town to bid a merchant come who will shortly bring silks and gay attire for the bride. An it please you, be merry, Marian; weddings come not oft at Weregrave, and it is meet you greet my tidings with greater joy," and she fell a-laughing, while I burst forth a blubbering like a silly mooncalf.

"If thou dost wed in thirty days, my lady, evil will surely fall, for that thy wedding will come i' the wane of the moon," saith I, twixt tears and choking.

"Thy superstition hath it right for once, Marian. An evil omen for an evil thing," saying which she passed to her chamber and bolted herself within, nor would she open or give heed all the day, though I did coax and my master storm. I was greatly feared that harm had befallen, so silent was all within, save when I laid mine ear 'gainst the panel I could hear her soft footfall on the floor, as she paced its length through the day and far into the night.

Not even when the silk merchant was come would she answer or open to us, despite that my master raged and threatened to burst the panel. Thus was it perforce thrust upon me to choose for her the rich silk for her wedding garment, which, God pardon, I felt as if 't were her shroud, and wept so I durst not come near the fabric lest my tears stain it and bring yet further ill to my love.

But when the next morn dawned, she bore herself calmly, and seemed to differ little from her old self save that a something of youthful graciousness was gone, and she had on a sudden passed from child to woman. She stood apart from all, even Marian, and I did bethink 't was as when a gardener doth on a sudden strip all support from a slender twig and leave it henceforth to stand alone, lashed by the storms of life.

Sir Hugh came not often to Weregrave in that month afore the wedding, nor seemed he desirous of speech alone with my lady withal; though she bore herself toward him with a steady quiet as unlike as maybe her usual whiffling mood. Belike 't was this that caused him discomfort in her presence. I think he did even fear her in those days, as the butcher fears the gaze of the lamb under his knife.

Then it was that Sir Ralph fell sick of a fever, which grew so grievous that after my lady had done all that might be, to no purpose, with simples and brews of her own making, she was frighted, and bade Giles take her own white mule and haste to the town six leagues distant, and fetch a barber; who, when he was come, straightway bled my lord.

Thus was the fever stayed for a time, and Sir Ralph was for being up within a few days at most; but I knew 'twas not to be, when he did take, on a Sunday before Saint Bart's day, a sudden turn for the better: for it be known to all that if one sick of a fever doth mend on the Lord's day, as well post for the priest and confess him with all speed.

Howbeit, my lady wot not of this, and I held my peace from telling her, she being greatly cheered.

The day of the wedding coming nigh, and her father still keeping him to his couch, she had hopes to push the time yet farther on; but my lord would hear naught of waiting, seeming the rather to wish for haste in the matter; and when my lady, breaking through her calm, did plead with him for delay, his anger mounted high, and straightway he fumed himself into a fever again. After this my lady durst say no more.

Thus was she wed, beside her dying father; Sir Hugh coming in brave array with the priest, who had need that day to wed a pair and shrive a soul.

My master would hear of naught but that my lady should wear the wedding garments which he had provided for her; so I myself arrayed her, while she stood as one without sight or hearing. Her surcote and mantle was of rich silk of Almeri, white, and wrought with powderings of silver, sown with pearls. Beshrew me, but Sir Hugh furnished forth the money for it, else it had not been bought, which I dare be sworn my lady wist, for she had never cast a glance upon it. Howbeit 't was the finest apparel that I had ere seen then. Now, God be thanked, my lady walks in just as grand on any day she pleaseth.

When all was in readiness I led her to the half ruined chapel of the Manor, where Giles and Clement and Henry had already borne my lord on his pallet, he looking more like dead than living man, and there was my lamb wed, while we stood around weeping as it were a burying.

Scarce had the priest finished the word that bound them, when my lady fell beside her father; for a great change was come over him, and the pinched look o' the nose and mouth, together with the grayness of his face, did speak him a dying man.

"My lord, my lord," she cried, "speak to me, I beseech thee. 'T is thy Joscelyn, thy little maid that calls. Father, oh my father, go not from me thus; forsake me not in mine anguish," saith she in tone of grievous pain; but he answered naught, and we thought his spirit sped. Then did she utter this mighty cry as to God, "Now am I utterly bereft," and fell a-swooning beside him. Thus when the men bore my master back to his couch, Sir Hugh did follow, my lady in his arms looking like a wounded white doe.

Such was her wedding; no feasting or dancing, no mirth or minstrelsy, only tears and sadness midst ruin and decay, which yet seemed best to agree with it.

My lord was not dead, though never again in this world came he to himself, but lay with eyelids close shut, a-breathing out his life in labored breaths, my lady, who was recovered from her swoon, sitting near, fondling his hand in hers, and giving him loving words: and I could see that she did hope still, for that a glimmer of life was in him. He labored with death till darkness fell, and a great storm, which had gathered all the day, burst with fury over the Manor, the wind lashing and howling like a demon spirit. Ever and anon, through the crash of the storm came borne to us, on waves of sound, the solemn boom of the soul bell, which tolled out through all that waiting time to aid my master's passing, and give him start of the evil spirits.[1]

[1] The passing bell, or soul bell, was commonly thought by the ignorant to be rung for the purpose of driving away the evil spirits who waited to seize the newly released soul. All evil spirits are supposed to be unable to endure the sound of a bell.

Suddenly bethinking me of the reason of his long struggle, I straight opened every casement and door in the Manor; then on a mighty rush of wind his spirit sped like a bird from a cage.[1]

I forced my lady gently away then, for she would not go of her own will, saying to me o'er and o'er, with soft smile, that her father slept and would soon waken.

She did not behold him again till he lay streeked and wrapped in his winding sheet, with the death lights burning about him, when I had much ado to keep her from letting fall her tears upon the corpse.[2]

Then came days I know not how to tell of, so confused is memory withal. My lady sat apart in her chamber, and took no heed of the coming and going about her; nor seemed she to see any upon whom her gaze rested. Beshrew me, but it made Sir Hugh's flesh creep to have her look on him as he were thin air and had no solid substance.

Scarce had I time for breathing then, for Sir Ralph's funeral feast must be furnished, and our larder as bare as a priest's cupboard on a fast day, and empty would the crowd have gone from our gates an it had not been that Sir Hugh sent to his manor and fetched thence

---

[1] The superstition is, that a soul cannot easily pass if any lock in the house be closed, or any bolt shot.

[2] It disturbed the ghost of the dead and was fatal to the living if a tear was allowed to fall on a winding sheet.

poultry and sheep and cattle, as well as cooks and serving people to prepare the same: nor did he stint him in wine and ale, but conveyed it to Weregrave in generous quantity. And the folk came flocking like evil birds, scenting death from afar, circling and soaring till they light on the feast: knights and gentlemen, yeomen and churls, jugglers, minstrels and tatterdemalions, came they all.

The baser sort caroused in the court, the minstrels singing, the jugglers doing tricks of tumbling, wrestling, and dexterity of hand, and all, whatsoever their sort, pouring the liquor into open throats and bottomless paunches. The knights and gentlemen Sir Hugh did entertain in the great hall, and here wine flowed as ale without in the courtyard.

When the hour of sepulture was come, I drew my lady to the lattice of her chamber, and together we watched my master's body borne forth on a bier, the heavy pall over it amost covering to the feet of the bearer. Eight men came after with torches aflame, and a company of brothers from the monastery chanted a mournful requiem. Sir Hugh walked next as nearest of kin, and the crowd followed, their coarse laughter hushed to decency for the moment. To the Manor chapel they bore him, the bell tolling in solemn stroke the while. There in the crypt 'neath the chancel they laid him, the last of his name.

Then was such a feast laid as Weregrave had not beheld since my memory. In the court the tables groaned 'neath pork flesh, oaten cake and cheese, with abundance of ale and mead to wet the fare. In the great hall, fowls, venison, beef, and whole sheep with bread of wheaten flour and butts of wine offered cheer to the better sort.

Long they sat carousing, Sir Hugh, at the table head, sending round the wine flagon did any falter. The light waned, and the torch men entered, bearing great flaming torches, which cast wanton shadows over the scene.

Many slept the night where they sat, fallen on the table in drunken stupor, and some scorned not to lay beneath, 'twixt the feet of their companions.

When the night was far spent, I saw Sir Hugh, heavy with wine, his face purple, his great under lip a-hanging, reel to my lady's chamber. Then prayed I, God be merciful to my lamb.

II

GODFREY'S TALE

Of a certainty, if it were my part to set down the chronicle of my wanderings in the Holy Land they are like never to be writ, despite that my lady hath commanded it, for I am but an indifferent scrivener, and my great hand hath an unskilful manner of missing hold of the penner and leaving a great botchery of black spots from the ink-horn upon finger and parchment. But and if thou hast work for me with the sword, withal, swift my blade flies from its sheath, the hilt nestling to my hand, and on the instant I am become a whole man.

I ofttimes ponder of that heaven which priest and church doth allow shall be a land where no fighting is, and my heart lieth heavy within me at thought that when I go hence, nevermore shall the hilt of my good sword loving leap to the hollow of my palm as wench to her sweetheart's breast. I am not used to pray greatly or oft, but at such times there doth creep to my lips, unawares, a little prayer that the King of heaven may be pleased to have some fighting for His warriors, and that He may maintain an army in heaven, even if it be but a little one. And I doubt not that 't will be so, despite priest and church, there having been dissension and war in heaven ere this; for thou canst not make me to believe there was not some tall fighting and good when Lucifer was put forth into hell.

But as I was for saying earlier, I am but to word this my tale to Anselm, who will set it down for me, he having as great ease with the penner and ink-horn as I with the sword.

I begin these happenings in the incarnate year of our Lord 1190, when Richard of England and Philip of France lay in camp at Messina. For it boots not that I tell thee of those heavy days when first I rode from Weregrave, leaving my heart netted in the golden hair of my lady; or of the assembling of the army at Tours, which place was come so crowded, after a time, with the multitude of people, that they did mightily inconvenience each other; or of how, therefore, by the king's command, a part of the royal fleet sailed to Messina, there to await his coming. 'T is enough to tell thee that 'mongst these first I went with my one squire, John o' Bardon, and a small company of men-at-arms, under my feudal lord, Roger Fitz Rainfrey.

Over all our journeyings I pass in haste, and come at once to that time when we had been many weeks at Messina, and to my meeting with a youth whose tale doth make so large a part of mine own that I am for thinking 't is more his story than mine which I am about to word.

'T was a street broil which first did bring the lad to my knowledge; not that sharp word and sharper blow were aught to catch thine ear, for these were troublous times, look you, and the sound of steel 'gainst steel, bemingled with the oaths and cries of the combatants were like to ring forth at any hour. For it be known to you, that not only was there quarrel and dissension 'twixt the Crusaders and the Lombards,[1] but such deep jealousies did ferment 'twixt Frenchman and Englishman, that the white and the red cross[2] were like to bear more ill toward each other than either toward the heathen crescent withal.

'T was plain to behold that the French king conceived himself — God help the while! — despitefully used for that Richard, being his vassal for Normandy, Gisors and Aquitain, did nathless so far exceed him in wealth and renown.

Philip was first come at Messina, and, disdaining all show, he made land without the

---

[1] It is probable that he calls this portion of the population Lombards because they were occupied in mercantile pursuits. They were not, of course, Lombards by nation.

[2] In this Crusade the English wore a white cross, the French a red.

pomp of sovereignty, contenting him with one vessel and the gentlemen of his household in attendance: Richard, remembering the proverb which doth say "Such as I see you are, I esteem you," and, moreover, being fully persuaded that the state of a king doth well grace him in the eyes of his subjects, made land in fashion seemly for so mighty a monarch.

When his coming was noised abroad throughout the city, the people laying aside their occupations ran together to the sea, so that a wall of faces did line the shore when the innumerable galleys swept into harbor, laden and adorned with various kinds of armor, together with countless standard and pennon a-floating in the breeze; 'til the galleys resembled naught so much as monstrous birds, having gaudy plumage and wings of white. The sea was made to boil with the number of oarsmen; trumpet and clarion spake with deafening sound. Lo! then the forward galleys did on a sudden sunder from each other, and swift as a bolt from an arbalest there shot forward the vessel which bore the king.

'Twas painted in divers colors, and everywhere most cunningly blazoned with the lions of England, the while the deck bristled with pennon and standard. On the prow of the vessel, under the banner of England, which the breeze did fling forth and toy with, as for love of it, stood my lord the king.

Godfrey's Tale

He was tall of stature, graceful in figure, his legs straight and flexible, his arms long, and not to be matched for wielding a sword. His hair did shade 'twixt red and auburn, and his eyes were a keen and piercing gray. The sunlight shone on his glittering armor, touching the white cross on his breast into silver. His royal mantle of green, laid back at the shoulder, showed a rich lining of vair.

The shout of the people mingled with the blare of the trumpets as the galleys came to land, and Richard, stepping forth, trod the path of rich cloth thrown down to the water's edge, to where his Cyprian bay horse, barbed and fretting, awaited him. Thus, girt about by knights and barons, on gaily caparisoned steeds, the king rode through the shouting multitude to his royal pavilion.

And from that hour there was begun that jealousy which gave rise to ill seeming and ill speaking, and made English and French ever ready to snatch at excuse for contention 'twixt each other, the while the Griffones sought constant occasion of injury to both parties, but more particularly the English, whom they hated for no cause, 'til our state was well-nigh beyond bearing, we being withheld from all save secret retaliation.

Much complaint of the Lombards, of their extortion and insult, was made to the king's ear, but he ever counselled patience, begging his knights and barons restrain their men: for that he desired to fight none save the enemies of the cross; with all others he would abide in peace and brotherly love. Notwithstanding, so much was come to him of injustice and wrong done, that he, perforce, demanded a council of peace, in which the chief justiciaries of the city of Messina were met, together with Richard and Philip.

'T was on the very hour of the sitting of this council in the great pavilion of King Richard, that I, coming alone through the city, did pass in a narrow way a youth, who, at the door of a shop, bargained, with a loud-mouthed callet, for a loaf of wheaten bread.

The clack of her scolding tongue followed me afar, and I bethought me the boy was like to have his ears split an he came not soon to agreement with her: for by my hearing he did dispute the heaviness of the loaf and threat to have it weighed.

Thereupon the foul slut redoubled her clatter and 'gan to lay on blows with fist as well as tongue an the youth came within reach of her — which I promise you he did but seldom, defending him from her attack with the flat of his blade, nor striking back, though he had sore provocation.

I marked the fray from afar, where the sound of the woman's screams had fixed my steps; but seeing the youth was open to no peril save of a torn cheek from the shrew's nails an she got near him, I was for pressing onward without more ado, when I beheld a band of Lombards coming adown the street, summoned, I doubt not, by the clamor. Straight they fell upon the lad, who now gave play with his blade in right good earnest, but to little purpose 'gainst such heavy odds.

"Now by faith," quoth I, "'t is time I lent a hand," and swift I ran toward the spot; but being a distance off, ere I was come to his assistance, the youth was overpowered and lay prone upon the earth, where one ruffianly Lombard did pound his head 'gainst a stone, so that the boy, if not dead, was like, at smallest, to carry for life a brain as addled as a six months' egg.

"Hold, villain, in the name of the king," quoth I, and I sprung in the midst of the rabble: but, ever mindful of the king's command, I did only smite the churl on the cheek with the flat of my blade, when rightly I should have spitted him thereon. "The youth hath done thee no despite," I did maintain; "he but bargained for bread with yon scolding jade, who hath set on him for naught. I bid thee in the king's name — "

At the which they put to silence my words by much loud and scurrile talk, and one cried that Richard was no king, no fighter of aught save heathen dogs, and that they feared him not.

Then mine anger flamed high. "Now, by St. George, thou shalt swallow my sword for that foul speech, and that without delay," quoth I, and I set upon him with a right good will. In my wrath I had forgot me that I was one 'gainst many, who, though not all armed, did fill the want by sticks and stones and quarter-staves. Nathless, I planted me over the youth's prostrate body and dealt out blow and thrust with such swiftness as I might, but I was hard bested, and like soon, in spite of cut and thrust, to take my place beside the fallen boy, when on mine ear there fell the joyous sound of quick coming footfalls, and a shout of "St. George, St. George! Down with the Lombards! Down with the cheating dogs!"

Never sounded music more sweetly on mine ear, as in a trice a troop of English men-at-arms rounded the turn of the street and fell on mine adversaries with lusty blows and true, 'til the pack gave back, and there stood, fearing to come on, yet loth to let be. Howbeit, 't was but an instant thus, for the clamor brought other citizens with each moment, and 't was plain we must make swift retreat an we hoped to reach camp with unbroken skins.

I raised the swooning lad from the earth, and gave command to my comrades that they fall back slowly, the while they kept well together.

The Lombards beholding us give way renewed the attack with fierceness, emboldened thereto by increasing numbers, and sticks and stones fell in such showers we were like to have broken pates in plenty to bear back with us. Thanks be to the Virgin, the city gate was not distant far, and the citizens scarce dare go beyond it, else our men, seeing us beset, had fallen on them and rent them in sunder.

Nathless the camp came none too soon for me, the youth on my shoulder seeming a twenty hundredweight ere I laid him down; while I was also come aware that I bled well from a knife-thrust in my left shoulder.

Reaching my tent, I 'posited my burden gently on mine own pallet, and made ready to leech his wounds. His head bore many evil bruises, but no skin break, and I was for opening his doublet to see if they had let light into his slight body with their villain knives, when his eyes unclosed, and he gazed on me in wonder, a-trying to raise himself from the couch the while.

"Who art thou? Where am I?" saith he, as one but half awakened.

"Let be; thou art in safe hands, and I am for seeing if those Lombard dogs have let light into thy young body," quoth I, striving to untruss the points of his doublet, and showing a mighty awkwardness thereat. He plucked my fingers from him a'most peevishly, and felt his body o'er with careful hand. "Nay, I have no cut; I bethink me I am whole; but some villain hath dealt me a foul blow on the pate. 'T is the last I do remember. Even now it doth roar and pain so that I scarce can think. Tell me, I pray thee, how came I hither?"

"Another time, fair youth: now, an thou art not wounded, best rest and sleep. The camp is astir, and I must away. Lie thou here in safety 'til I come again, then shalt thou know all," saying which I hurried without, where the tale of our encounter had sped through the camp as fire over a stubble-field. It reached the great pavilion where the kings sat in council, no whit the smaller for that it had passed from mouth to mouth.

'T was afterward told me, that terms of peace were a'most agreed to, when one came with the tale that the citizens had set upon King Richard's soldiers without cause, and had ruthlessly slaughtered many of them.

Hearing which the king's wrath burned high, and he came to his feet on the instant, these words upon his lips:

"I have cried peace, peace, but there is no peace; now will I cry war." Then turning him to the justiciaries of the city, he commanded, "Go you, my lords, get you within your city gates with all the speed ye may, and say to the Lombards that Richard comes shortly to chastise them for every insult which he hath received of them."

At the which the King of France spake,

"Nay, nay, cousin, let not thy hasty tongue undo all our council hath so laboriously wrought. Patience, patience, I beg thee."

"My lord of France, too much of patience ill becomes a monarch, and most so when evil doth touch his subjects. The shortest way to peace oft lies through war; such seemeth now the case."

At which Philip held his speech, lifting only his brows as to say, "What use to try the curb on so evil a temper." For be it known to you, Philip was ever cautious in speech and act, never doing aught over-speedily; fearing nothing more than to repent him, he considered the result of everything before the commencement. Not so Richard. If injustice or oppression come to his ear, an he lose both life and kingdom, he will not stay 'til he right it.

Thus it was, that scarce had I stepped from my tent ere de Rancon, one of the king's gentlemen, laid hand on my shoulder, and bade me at once to the royal pavilion, where I was shortly brought into the presence of his majesty, who stood, a deep and angry frown upon his brow, and fretting impatience in his every look, whilst two knights did lace him in his armor.

When I assayed to go upon my knee, he bade me have done.

"Up from thy knee, man; this be no time for court mummery. Rather answer me this,

Sir Knight — for by thy collar and spurs I see thou art a knight — could'st not find meeter use for thy blade than in fomenting and abetting a common street broil? Canst not seek enough of quarrel with thine own sort to give thee thy bellyful at fighting, that thou must needs pit thy sword and lance 'gainst partisan and quarterstaff as well?"

At which the blood mounted to my head, and I held me as high as the king himself while I made answer:

"By my vow of knighthood, your majesty, am I most solemnly pledged to uphold the cause of the innocent and defend the weak from oppression. This have I done; no more. Richard himself, an he had been there, had not done less."

"By my faith, thou seemest oversure of the justice of thy cause. Word thy tale as it happened, and see thou dost not give it partisan coloring, and if it be as thou sayest, Richard will cry thee pardon, and name himself overhasty in his reproving."

Whereupon I unfolded my tale, each happening as it was, 'til when the end was nigh I saw that the king's eye had changed from sternness to commendation.

"Thou hast done right well, Sir Knight, and thy king was over-hasty of speech;" saying which, he brought his great hand down with friendly force upon my shoulder — which it being the left one, and sore wounded, I did flinch from the pain like as a silly wench. "How now," saith he, "blood! thou art hurt;" then, with a look full of whimsey, "I do bethink me thy king is but a clumsy fellow, all said, since in seeking to heal the wound his hasty tongue hath wrought his hand doth inflict yet another."

"Nay, sire, 't is but a scratch from a Lombard's knife, and scarce worthy thought. I knew not of it 'til I reached the camp."

"What is thy name?" he did question me.

"Godfrey de Bersac, your majesty."

"And thy feudal lord?"

"Roger Fitz Rainfrey; there be none worthier," quoth I, with something of pride.

"Thou sayest true. Go you in haste, seek out Fitz Rainfrey, say that, by the king's command, you fight this day near our royal person. Then arm thee at once and return thither. We will in the hour teach those Lombard dogs a new note to tongue. Nay, nay, no thanks; 't is but thy due. Waste not the moments in words; thou shalt act thy gratitude."

Never armed I more gaily, and there was scarce time for the winking of an eyelid, ere I was mounted on my destrier and back with the king's guard.

We marched forth ten thousand strong that day — knights, men-at-arms, and bowmen — for the French king joined not with us in this quarrel, but retired to his lodgings within the city, where it hath been said he most treacherously urged on the Griffones, and did even assist in the defence in so far as he dared.

'Gainst a fenced city of fifty thousand folk we marched; and, had our cause been other than just, never had we gained the day.

The attack was opened by our long-bow and cross-bowmen, who advanced, well covered by pavisse and mantelet — which, heaven be witness, they had need of 'gainst the cloud of bolts and arrows which soon flew from the city walls, like a flock of ill-omened birds.

'T was my first battle, and, in the hot ignorance of youth, I raged much at seeing our archers skulk in the shadow of their defence, and return so poor an answer to the challenge of the Lombards: but when I fumed forth my wrath to Gerard Talbot, who rode a-near me, he chid my unacquaintance with the art of warfare.

"Thou art over-new at this game, as, indeed, it seemeth to me the Lombards be also, else wouldst thou know our men but draw their fire. When the enemy's claws are cut, thou 'lt see the English know how to rain bolt, quarrel, and arrow, as hail on a summer day."

And so it proved; for when the besieged had somewhat exhausted them, then did our archers let fly, and such a cloud darkened the sky, that for a brief space the walls were left without guard, for that one could not so much as look out of doors, but he would have an arrow in his eye ere he could wink it.

This occasion did our men seize upon, and a frail bridge of plank was thrown across the moat. Over swarmed the soldiers, and in less time than I can speak it, a scaling ladder was a-fixed to the wall, and a half a score of knights on it, with shields held overhead to guard 'gainst the great stones hurled down on them from above. Ranulf de Roveirie led the assault, and it was with heart a'most betwixt my teeth that I beheld him mount even to the battlements; when, the scaling ladder, on a sudden being half loosened from its hold by a cursed Lombard on the wall, swung to the side, and flung our men to the earth with awful force.

But first had Ranulf grappled with his enemy above, whom he did hold fast, dragging him over the wall, the two falling to the earth, clinched in so mighty a death grip, that, when our men did assay to raise the Norman knight and bear him to a place of safety, they needs must take his companion also.

The trumpets sounded; our men fell back; the archers engaged the enemy anew, clearing the wall as before. Again did knights and men-at-arms assault, to be again beaten back, though the king was himself in the midst, directing and cheering.

Once more we retired; then did the king make command to the archers that they renew the attack, and when all was in readiness assault again with all the force possible, but at every hazard, keep the enemy in play 'til they did hear his trumpet blast from the other side of the city. "Then," saith he, "come with all the speed ye may, for I will have forced an entrance to the town."

Then took he with him fifty knights, one of whom I was, and as many of bowmen and men-at-arms, and with all caution, and as secretly as we might, we rode, skirting a low hill, which did cut us from the view of those upon the wall. Thus were we able to come upon the other side of the city, where there was situate an old and ill-guarded postern, of which my lord the king had ta'en cognizance some few days agone.

When we were well advanced from the cover of the hill, and come in sight of the handful of bowmen upon the wall, consternation did seize upon them, and they sounded forth the alarm — but to little purpose, for that the body of our troops did so press on the other wall of the city as to keep them most fully engaged. They also let fly right gallantly at us with bolt and quarrel, but our bowmen shortly saw to it that none dare look abroad an he were not prepared to take leave of his life; and the wall being thus cleared, a great battering ram was set up over against the postern, the king himself directing its preparation.

Then the crash of the ram, the cracking of heavy but rotted timbers; again the men ran back for yet another blow; this time Richard himself guided its force. Ere long the postern lay in splinters, offering little resistance to our progress.

'T was then that a monstrous blast echoed from our trumpets, and an answering shout of "St. George, St. George for merrie England!" came faintly to us, and we ware they had hearkened to our signal.

Our little band pressed through the postern and grappled in hand-to-hand conflict with the Lombards.

Now the fight raged fiercely, and I know naught save that I gave and took blow on blow, as it seemed, for hours, though it could scarce have been a score of minutes ere the English 'gan pouring through the postern, and the Lombards to flee, seeking refuge in the houses, on the roofs, and in the solars, from whence they harried us much by hurling upon us stones and heavy articles of whatsoever sort.

The desire to hack, to hew, to kill — *to kill* — did so possess me that I fought on, following the flying, drenched in mine own blood, knowing no pain, feeling no tire, 'til I did on a sudden encounter in the way the same villain who in the morn had set upon the youth, and uttered to mine ear that foul insult to my lord the king.

"Well met, thou costrel Lombard," I shouted joyously; "I was withheld this morn of my purpose towards thee, by strength of circumstance. Now will I have an accounting with thee for thy insult to the king. Defend thyself, villain, an thou want not to go unhousled to thy grave," quoth I.

"If thou art verily the English ban-dog who was so fierce at my throat this morn because of thy wounded pup, I'll e'en give thee to know thou art more like than I to go hence unhousled," saying which he did cross blades with me, and we 'gan to fight in right good earnest.

Something of truth was there in his vaunt, he being no mean swordsman for a spent and wounded man to fall foul of, — both of which I now came aware I was, as I parried his keen, quick thrust, and assayed to give as good. Twice did I break down his guard, and twice did he recover him with agile move, and I was for thinking I had underta'en more than I was like to carry forward, when, by the help of the Holy Virgin, the Lombard — who had given back some paces as we fought — slipped in a slime of cooling blood, which oozed from a dead soldier fallen in a heap on the doorway of a nearby house.

Mine adversary lay prone at my feet ere he knew what was befallen him, and, my foot on his breast, I set the point of my blade 'gainst his teeth. Looking on me thus, his face paled to a ghastly whiteness, and his eyes started from his head in horrid fright. I bethought me how near spent was I, and how 't was but a chance which did place him there, and, despite that he was but a stinking Lombard, he had fought with no mean skill; thinking all of which I was ware I had no stomach for to carry out my threat.

"By St. Hilary," quoth I, "I like not this task. Beshrew me, neither wilt thou when thou comest to it; for my trusty blade will give thee an indigestion thou art like never to recover from, and good meat will have little flavor for thy tongue henceforward. If thou 'lt name thyself a lying dog in thine insult to my lord the king, I 'll e'en give thee a good kicking and let thee go free of the feast I have made ready for thy swallowing."

He did eye me a long second; then, in sour tone, consented him to my terms, and named himself, as I commanded, at the which I bestowed upon him the kicking which I had pledged — though it was over mild, I being so totty I scarce could stand. Then I bade him begone, which he straightly did, without tarrying.

And thus did King Richard capture Messina by one assault, in less time than a priest could chant the matin service.

Never felt I greater joy at sight of my couch than when I was come again within mine own tent. So spent was I from fatigue and loss of blood that I had much ado to stay upright on my destrier-back as we rode into camp.

When my squire had unharnessed me, and bathed and bandaged my wounds pouring a healing balsam thereon, I fell on a long and deep sleep, from which I came not to myself 'til the next day's sun was high in the heaven. Nor, do I bethink me, I had then wakened save that a light hand touched my shoulder, and a gentle voice, whose tone spake fear, sounded on mine ear: "My lord, my lord," it said; and when my lids unclosed, I beheld a pair of grieving eyes fixed on me, whose look straight turned to joy at my awakening.

"Dear my lord, I cry you pardon for my unmannerliness; but thou didst breathe so faintly, and thou hast slept so long and deeply, that fear seized on me, it seeming that thou must be a-passing in thy slumber. I thank the saints 't is not so," saith he.

"Amen to that, say I, for I have scant wish to part thus early from a world so full of good living and joyous fighting. If memory doth not trick me, thou art the lad whom the Lombards did so cruelly mistreat this morn," quoth I.

"Nay, thou hast slept many hours. 'T was yestermorn that thou didst bring me hither, for which act I do render thee a full and greatful heart," saith he.

"How dost thou find thyself this day, good youth: none the worse despite thy pounding?" I made question of him.

"Not so, my lord," he did avow with rueful countenance. "I yet bear a mighty mount of soreness on my pate, and a body which doth lament and complain grievously an I move it. But, gramercy to thee, I wear no broken bones."

"It doth appear to me that thou art over-grateful for small service. Now shalt thou acquaint me of thy name; then begone to thine own lord, who will be for thinking thee dead. If thou hast ever need of friend, remember Godfrey de Bersac, who owes it to thee that he hath this day come under the king's eye," quoth I, making ready to turn again to slumber.

"Stay yet a moment, my lord, for I have favor to beg of thee on the instant. My name is Ronald de Glanville, and the life which thou hast rescued at risk of thine own doth belong to thee. I would I could enter thy service, Sir Godfrey," quoth he.

"Nay, that may not be, for many reasons, good youth, — the first and greatest being the king's own law, which doth forbid a change of service to any unless his master agreeth thereunto. Then thou must know, I have a'ready one squire who doth serve me with reasonable diligence," I made answer.

"To thy first objection, I beg thee know,

naught stands 'twixt me and my desire save thine own will. I am of the following of Ranulf de Roveirie, who, as thou art doubtless already ware, was slain yestermorn in the assault on the city. To thy second saying I make answer, two squires are not over many to serve a knight such as thou."

"Aye, thou sayest true, two squires be not over many for a gentleman, but and if he be a poor beggar of a knight. What say you then? May not one mouth the more be over many for him to feed and look to?"

"Nay, but I'll cost thee naught; and 't is little I need at greatest, and I'll e'en furnish forth thy rough camp fare in such savory fasbion, thou 'lt be for thinking that thou dost sit at meat at the king's board. Say thou 'lt let me bide with thee, my lord, and such loving service shall be thine as thou hast not so much as dreamed on ere this:" 't was thus he pled with me, his eyes aglow, his cheek flushed.

"But thou art over young for a squire. How many years hast thou?"

"Twenty, come next St. Hilary's day, my lord," quoth he proudly.

"Nay, nay, good youth, an thou please me thou must bear a truth-speaking tongue, above all. By thy look and bearing thou canst scarce carry more than fifteen summers." I passed my fingers over his chin, which, as a body might say, was as soft as a silken doublet. "Beshrew me, a cat could e'en act the barber to thee, didst thou but lave thy face with cream," quoth I, a-laughing.

At the which he turned a mighty color of red, and drooped his head in shame.

"Look ye, Ronald, droop not thy bright head thus; I meant not to put thee to shame, for I bethink me thou didst play the man right gallantly yestermorn when thou wast set upon by those cursed Lombards. I did but chide thee for that thou wert over ready to desire extra weight of years. Forget it not, boy, age will press hard enough on thy heels, be thou as fleet as the thought of man, and he will o'ertake ere thou likest without loitering or coaxing o' thine. Speed before the villain, 'tis the only foe brave men may fly; the foe who of a certainty shall o'ercome all at the last. Now go you, leave me to further slumber; when I waken I'll ponder thy wish, and if thou art still of a mind to take service with a poor knight when thou couldst fare richly with some powerful baron, then I'll to the king and gain his consent to keep thee," and I turned once more to slumber.

'T was past the hour of nones ere I wakened, so refreshed in body that I rose from my couch, bathed, and ate a supper great enough for three men such as be I.

The boy having still the same mind — and of a truth I was glad it should be so — I then sought the king, and was shortly admitted to his presence.

Supper was but now over, and his majesty still sat at the board. Cup and flagon told why he lingered. A minstrel seated near touched his harp, and discoursed in melting tones a ballad of love and war.

The king made sign that I be silent 'til the song was done. I obeyed, waiting the last sad strain, which died on the air ere I kneeled before his majesty.

"Nay, not there: up, man, and say thy say a-standing. I trow thou art too good a soldier to be fair courtier withal. What wouldst thou have of us?" he did question.

"Let me be here on my knee, my lord, for I am come to crave a boon of thee," quoth I.

"If thou art for seeking favors, make thy request large, Sir Knight, for I am in generous humor, and like to grant aught in reason."

"Gramercy for thy goodness, your majesty, but I'll not press hard on thy favor in this. I but crave leave to take into my service the youth whose tale I unfolded to thee yestermorn. His lord, Ranulf de Roveirie, is slain — God rest his soul! — and the boy being full of foolish gratitude doth greatly desire to abide with me."

"Said I not that thou wouldst be but an indifferent courtier, else hadst thou grasped the occasion to ask of me a fair estate at smallest. Let be as thou sayest; keep the youth, and welcome. But how art thou placed? Canst thou provide with ease for another squire?" he did demand of me.

"As to that, your majesty, I have showed him my state and represented to him 't were wiser he sought service with some powerful baron; but he is still of the same wish, and I'll not deny I am pleased at having it thus, there being something in his look and bearing which doth mightily commend itself to me," quoth I.

"So let it be, then, and I will see to it that thou hast a fair share of yesterday's plunder, which shall help thee meet the expense of thine enlarged household." Then with his own hand he filled a drinking flagon, which handing to me, saith he, "Empty this draught, Sir Godfrey, to as hasty a conquest of Saladin and his heathen host as yestermorn we made of the Griffones;" and together we drained the vessels to the last drop.

'Twas not 'til many months after, that our forces drew out of Messina. The winter was spent and spring well come ere our galleys moved from harbor, and much dissension and some fighting lay between.

To knights like myself, who rejoiced not in great store of gold, this long continued idleness worked grievous hardship, our poor means being well nigh exhausted. Moreover were we called upon after the signing of peace with King Tancred, to restore to the citizens of Messina the plunder taken from them in the sack of the city.

Richard, seeing the hardship this worked to us, did of his generosity give freely to those of his knights who had need; but, withal, we fared hardly enow toward the end of our tarrying, and great impatience was manifest at the long delay.

The boy Ronald kept fully his pledge to render me most loving service. Such poor fare as we came by, he set forth in so savory a guise thou wouldst scarce have guessed its plain beginnings.

I ever strove to fend the youth from our most grievous hardships, and if, perchance, some dainty gobbet came to my hand, 't was for him I put it by. Despite that he seemed hardy, nor ever uttered complaint, I could not rid me of the thought that he was most tender of body. He was ever brave, and bore himself knightly; no broiler, yet ready with his blade when the occasion made demand; but, withal, I could not turn me from the thought that he was not unlike a delicate wench, and that the indomitable spirit within did animate at once and consume him.

When every service which lay to his hand had been freely rendered, and there seemed naught to give occasion for work, he would fall on my armor and rub and rub upon the steel 'til it shone as the sun. On a day, he working thus, softly warbling a pretty note the while, I stretched upon my couch, a-watching him, he upheld before mine eyes the glittering chamfron of my destrier. Saith he, laughing, "See how it doth gleam! By my faith, 't is as bright as the silver platter from which the king doth feed;" at which I fell a-gibing him. "I could a'most be sworn, at times, that thou art a wench, so womanlike is thy speech, Ronald. Say, rather, it doth shine as the sun, the lightning, or aught save a silver platter. Nay, blush not nor look shamed, lad. Thy speech may be wench-like, but I mind me thou art ever ready to play the man with thy blade;" then, on this instant, I beheld him take my helmet, and 'gin with dexterous touch to unlace the cord which bound over it a silk mesh net. I sprung in haste to catch his wanton fingers.

"Stay, boy, hold thy presumptuous hand. By St. Hilary! if thou hadst ta'en off that net thou and I had parted company in a twinkling. Never touch thy hand to it an thou want not sharp words and ill looks from thy master."

"But the helmet is tarnished to a shameful dulness, and I may not cleanse it an I take not off the net," he did protest.

"Then let be; it weareth enough of brightness over it," quoth I with firmness.

He sat with downcast look, nor uttered aught for a long space, and I was for thinking that my impatient threat had grieved his loving heart. I had mended my fault with a word, but, upon opening my mouth to give speech, he brake silence with sudden question, in tone as unlike as might be to that which he was wont to use.

"'T is a lady's favor?" saith he.

"Thou sayest true," I made answer, and again was he silent, while I thought on her so far hence, whose loving hand had placed the token there, saying, the while she did it, in tone which doth still abide in mine ear, "Wear it, Godfrey, 'til thou come again."

"Is she fair to look on?" Ronald's voice broke on my tender musing.

I smiled soft, remembering her. "England doth boast none more beautiful."

"And thou dost love her?" On this time there was a sharp ring in the tone as if somewhat did pain him.

"I have not words to tell how much," quoth I solemnly.

Then again silence fell, while Ronald put by the helmet, eyeing it as 't were an evil thing which he fain would ne'er touch henceforward. After a space he broke forth in a voice of great dolor, "When thou art come again to England thou 'lt have no need for Ronald," at which I fell a-laughing.

"By the Holy Rood, I trowe thou art passing jealous of my love for a maid. Foolish boy!" and I laid my hand upon his bended head; "thou shalt go back with me to England and be my lady's page. In the light of her dear eyes thou'lt think no more of love for thy rough master; then will my hour for jealousy be come."

"Dost think a woman's eyes could turn my heart from thee?" saith he, in tones of scorn.

"Aye, that do I, with so sudden a veering thou'lt scarce tell the instant. But wait a short space; thou'lt have a love of thine own, then shalt thou know of a power thou canst not now conceive," quoth I, a-shaking my head wisely.

"I shall never have a love as others," saith he, rising from his work, and making him ready to depart.

"Now thou art prating as a graybeard who is done with youth. Thou canst know naught of these things, being in the green spring of thy boyhood."

Thereupon he turned and sent into mine eyes a look which longed to utter somewhat, yet most ardently desired a withholding of the same, — a look which did beseech me know, yet did command me not dare dream. This troubled me greatly, and I sat long pondering what might be on the child's heart.

But as I did say, awhile back, the spring broke at last, and our galleys put to sea. With the fleet sailed Queen Johanna, sister of the king, accompanied by Berengaria, the daughter of the King of Navarre, who was shortly to be wedded with Richard.

When we were but two days distant from land a terrible storm broke, the waves lashing and tossing our light crafts like as they were bubbles, and many were for thinking we would ne'er see solid earth again; and some there were, I trowe, who cared little an we did not. For the tossing hither and thither of the ship had caused with these so great a feeling of unrest in the paunch that they cared for naught save to be dead or whole of their sickness.

The night fell, and, the storm still raging, King Richard caused to be hoisted on the galley which bore him a monstrous lanthorn burning a great wax candle, which sent forth a light far over the water, hoping that thus we might be enabled to keep somewhat anear one another. 'T was without avail; the wind served us as it listed.

When the dawn broke, scarce one half of the fleet were to be seen; neither as the day wore on and the storm dropped did they come to sight, and many hearts were heavy, for that the king's galley was among the number of those missing.

Our fears grew yet in heaviness when we

were come at last to land at the city of Acre, for the king was not arrived there before us as we did hope.

But here found we the King of France, who had sailed from Messina three weeks afore us, encamped against the city, together with the Dukes of Austria, Burgundy, and Flanders, also the Knights Hospitallers and the Knights Templars.

Long had the siege endured ere France came to Acre, and the troops were faint of heart and weak of arm. This were little to be marvelled at, seeing that for a space food had e'en been so scarce that there were many who all but starved; a state, withal, in no wise better for lusty fighting than is an over-abundance, which doth surfeit a man and make him heavy with sloth.

'Twas said that ere the provision ship came, which relieved their dire need, that many gnawed and ate the dirty bones already mouthed by the dogs, others feeding them on grass; and that the starving men struggled and fought at the ovens for the scant bread baked as they had been beasts. This famine, together with the great fall of rain, did breed grievous sickness amongst the men, who died in scores.

Then had come the ship bearing food, shortly followed by the King of France; and the near hope of having the valiant King of England; and faint heart took hope and drooping courage revived.

Just here it appeareth well to give some description of this city so famous for its magnificence as well as the various incidents of war. Acre hath the form of a triangle, narrow on its western side. Howbeit, it extends in wider range toward the east, and hath a full third part washed by the ocean on the south and west. The port, which is not so convenient as should be, oft deceives and proves fatal to the mariners who winter there; for the rock which lies over against the shore, to which it runs parallel, is too short to protect them from the fury of the storm. Upon this rock, it being a suitable place for washing away the entrails, 't is said the ancients were used to offer up sacrifices, and because of the flies, which ever follow the sacrificial flesh, the tower there standing is called the Tower of Flies.

About the city wall, as I have afore said, lay encamped the Christian host; and yet again beyond these lay the Turkish army, not in a compact body, but covering the mountains and valleys, hills and plains with tents, whose divers colors seemed to turn valley and hillside into a garden of monstrous great flowers.

Between the Turks and themselves had the Christians dug a trench to guard 'gainst surprise from without, while yet they kept constant watch lest there be a sudden sortie from the city.

Philip had caused his mangonels and petrarie

to be erected, and but awaited the coming of his brother-in-arms ere he struck the first blow.

'T was deemed expedient that the great fosse which surrounded the city of Acre should be filled, thus enabling the soldiers the more readily to charge the walls when mangonel and petrarie had effected a breach.

The common soldiers fell on this task with awakened zeal, nor did knight and squire disdain to lend aid, fetching the earth on their shields, whilst even devoted Christian women joined together in this rough service, bearing such small portions of earth as they might in their caught-up kirtles.

Not a few lives were lost in this labor, for the Turks spared not to have bowmen upon the walls to pick off the Christians with a constant flight of venomous arrows. One woman there was who fell in this service, struck in the side by the arrow of some villain Turk. Ere her soul was sped she begged a favor of the soldiers standing by, which came to be a mighty example of devotion to the army.

Saith she, breathing even now most faintly, for she was nearly passed, "Since, not being man, I cannot give of my strength in this struggle, I beseech you let my weakness avail somewhat: lay my body in the fosse. 'T will e'en save the labor of fetching so much of earth; and when the tramping feet of our men shall surge over this poor clay, surely my still heart will pulse, and I shall be satisfied, knowing I also serve."

Day followed unto day, bringing to us no news of Richard; and great fear and heaviness fell on all for thinking of the loss of this great king and greatest soldier.

Every morn scanned I the sea for long hours, hoping, perchance, to sight his sail; and every morn turned I away with hope yet sicker in my breast.

'Twas during this time of waiting that the Turks took on them ways of insolent boldness. Relying upon the exceeding swiftness of their horses, they made sudden and frequent sallies against our camp, killing some, and carrying away captive many who unwitting strayed too far from shelter. Seeing which, we deemed it expedient to prepare foot-traps, well concealed in the earth, which were mightily successful, and put a sudden end to their boldness.

'Twas thus I caught in a foot-trap of mine own making the horse, Mohammed; his rider, deeming it greater wisdom to part with horse than head, escaped, leaving the beast behind. Being of a build too slight to bear my heavy bulk, I did bestow him upon Ronald. Never saw I a more pleasing animal. His hair was more shining than a peacock's plumage; his head was lean, his eye gray like a falcon's, his breast large and square, his crupper broad and his rump tight. For speed he outmatched the thought of man, and withal was as gentle and loving as the lad who bestrode him.

The love and understanding betwixt the two was a marvel to behold. Ronald was alway for talking to him and treating him as man and Christian, and, beshrew me, the beast did appear to act as one at times.

Despite that our board was none so well provided, Ronald, of his scant fare, would each day lay by a gobbet of barley bread or oaten cake wherewith to coax the beast to frolic.

"Wilt thou have it, Mohammed?" the lad would question, holding aloft the morsel; at which the beast would make answer with little waves of joyful whinnying. "Then shalt thou salute thy master first;" thereupon would the horse rub his nose, now up, now down, 'gainst the lad's cheek, 'till he, holding one arm over the beast's neck the while, fed him the bit of bread. Which, having eaten, Mohammed of his own will would then bestow much fond nosing on the boy's face.

"By my faith, thou art as fond of the beast as 't were thy love," quoth I, as I watched their pretty fooling.

"'T is the only love that I shall ere possess," saith he; and once again there flashed within his eyes the look on which I spake afore.

At length, as thou knowest right well, Richard and his galleys were safely come to

Acre from Cyprus, where they had perforce tarried to give the inhospitable king of that isle a lesson he was not like to forget, since it brought him shackled in silver chains in King Richard's retinue.

'T was on a Saturday before the festival of the blessed Apostle Barnabas, in the Pentecost week, that Richard made land at Acre, and the earth trembled and dindled with the shouts of the acclaiming people. And look ye, Philip of France himself went to the shore to greet his brother-in-arms, and did conduct him with a great show of ceremony to the pavilion a'ready set for him; but 't was plain to behold, nathless, he little liked the joy with which the English king was made welcome. The day was kept as a jubilee, and universal gladness reigned throughout the army. Beshrew me, 't was little hard to say who held the love of the people. All through the day and far into the night — when it was fallen in a calm which seemed to smile on our undertaking — could be heard the clang of trumpet, the shrill sound of horns, the deeper note of harp and timbrel. Some there were who sung ballads, others drank, others yet played at club, kayles and such like games, each joying in his own fashion. The camp was alight with flaring torches, so that night became as day, and the Turks were doubtless for thinking the whole valley was consuming with fire.

Godfrey's Tale

But now must I pass hastily over the taking of the city of Acre, the preparations for which began in right good earnest after Richard's arrival; for it is not my desire to make this tale a chronicle of war, nor of those happenings, which being so well known to all, it hath the seeming of a waste of ink and parchment to recount the same. Rather is it my wish to give you the tale of mine own wanderings, and something of the adventures which fell to me the while.

So will I take up my story once more at the time when the armies of the Cross lay encamped in an olive grove on the thither side of the well-nigh ruined city of Joppa.

'Twas far within the month of September, though the sun burned upon us with a heat which it hath not at midsummer in England, and the army was but a wasted handful as set over against the host which erstwhile lay outside of the besieged city of Acre.

For all the world doth know of that most sad and shameful happening which befell the united armies of Christendom: how the King of France turned him and left the field so soon as the city of Acre was taken. How, with hand on the plow and the furrow scarce begun, he looked back, and forthwith gave over the task to which he had set him, urging, as a reason therefor, that his bodily health did not allow of his tarrying. By my faith, he had a right lusty look for so ill a man; and had he given over his spleen 'gainst King Richard, I dare be sworn he had been as strong as any.

When word of this desire came first to Richard's ear 't was said he would not hearken to that which he held to be a sorry jest; nor, 'til 't was forced on him, believed he that his brother in-arms of a truth desired to give up ere a blow had scarce been struck.

He struggled 'twixt anger and sorrow as he bade the lords who bore him this word return to King Philip, and say to him that the French were as the children of Ephraim, "who, being harnessed and carrying bows, turned themselves back in the day of battle."

Nathless, in the end, Richard must needs let him go, though 't was with grievous sorrow and shame for him.

Philip set sail, leaving a part of his force divided, some being under Count Henry of Champagne and some under the Duke of Burgundy.

It doth at times come to me, in looking backward, that it had been better for the hopes of Christendom an the French king had stayed within his own kingdom. In sooth, I do think he let and hindered the undertaking far more than he furthered it.

After the fall of Acre, King Richard was for pressing on 'gainst Jerusalem; and such terror had our arms a'ready struck 'mongst the heathen that I doubt not we had readily taken the holy city. But Philip would not, and Richard thus burdened — as a cat with a hammer tied to its tail — could not. Blessed Mary! 't is little use now to grieve of that which might have come to pass. Of our march to Joppa 'neath burning suns, harassed by the Turks, to whom we were at length forced to give battle, and whom, through the grace of God and by strength of our own right arm, we o'ercame 'gainst fearful odds, I say naught, but begin my tale from the time when we had a'ready been many weeks in camp, while the soldiers rebuilt the defences of the city of Joppa.

These days of waiting told heavily on our spirits; but most did they chafe and fret our impatient but noble king, who daily beheld the French turning back to the city of Acre, where ease did invite and pleasure entice them. In vain did Richard urge the leaders that they march against Askelon, which, even at that hour, was being despoiled and laid low by the Turks, that it might fall useless into our hand. None heeded, and there was left for him naught save to fume and fret as a snared beast, 'til, the time for such sport being come, the king 'gan to go a-hawking, which did something lighten his heavy mood.

On the day of which I would tell thee he rode from camp attended by a small body of knights, thinking him not to stray far. I well recall, whilst I equipped me by the king's command to accompany the hunt, I was 'ware that each move which I did make about the tent found Ronald at my heel, 'til, being something choleric that morn, I chid him soundly.

"What ails thee, boy, that thou art close on my heel each step I make as thou wert a suckling moon-calf and I thy dam. Beside the which, thy face hath the length of my sword. Hath any served thee ill? Say thy say quickly, for I have small time for child's fooling!"

"Nay, my lord, naught has befallen me. I scarce am ware myself of that which weighs upon my spirit—save—only—that—" and he grew hesitant, as if fearing to pursue his speech.

"What hast thou on thy tongue, boy? Word it, word it;" for by this thou 'lt see that the long waiting 'neath hot suns had of a truth done naught to sweeten mine own temper, which was ever something sour.

"I know not how to word it, master, save that I would thou wert not riding with the king this morn."

Whereupon I rounded on the boy:

"Why hast thou such thought in thy silly pate? Hast heard talk of treachery? Speak it an thou hast."

At hearing which Ronald's mood lightened

somewhat, and a little sorry smile stole to his mouth.

"By St. Hilary, my lord, dost think an I had I would stand thus dumb in thy presence? My fears are such as thou art wont to gibe at, which being so, it shamed me to utter them."

At which I fell a-laughing for the rueful look on the boy's countenance.

"Thou hast been a-dreaming again, hast thou?" I made question, for, be it known to you, Ronald was monstrous given to dreaming superstitious dreams, by which he did essay to foretell or interpret great happenings to the army; and 'twas ever my habit to scoff at and rate him not a little for this folly. Now that the secret was out he burst forth with a mighty sense of relief.

"Beshrew me, my lord, that I have, and such heavy dreams they were I greatly fear some danger threatens thee."

At which I fell a-laughing a second time, 'til the grieved look in the boy's eyes at length did stay me, despite my mirth. Saith I, striving then to give him comfort:

"And if it be so, Ronald, what recks it? Hath not the shadow of death lain these many days athwart our threshold? Art thou not yet come accustomed to his grim face? A soldier wakes not to any day an danger does not threat him, nor lies he down any night wherein danger doth not lurk anear. And wouldst thou have me to be frighted with the shadow of thy sleeping thoughts?"

For all answer the boy caught my hand a second to his cheek with a motion of tenderness, which sometimes he did allow himself and as straightly repent on in quick shamefacedness.

Despite my words, Ronald's mood was little lightened; and when I had mounted my destrier, and turned toward the spot whence the winding of horns told of the assembling hunt, I looked back to see the lad leaning his head most lovingly 'gainst the shining neck of Mohammed, and gazing after me with so grieving and fearsome a look in the depths of his eyes, that 'twas a time ere I could drive the same from my memory.

Nathless the morn passed swiftly, the dogs raising scant game. I bethink me the king had scarce loosed his falcon from his fist twice i' the time. We had also wandered far from camp, despite that we had thought not to. Thus, when coming on a spot where bush and tree afforded slight shelter from the burning sun, the king declared him a-weary and commanded us dismount and rest.

Then out spake Gerard Talbot; saith he: "My lord, I beg thee know we are yet many miles distant from camp, and like to be set upon by some wandering band of Saracens. I pray thee hold thy weariness yet a little, 'til thou art more safely situate."

"By the Holy Rood, but it doth appear that the hot sun of the East hath turned thy knightly heart to running water, that thou art on a sudden grown so fearsome," quoth the king, with a smile.

"Something of fear will be pardoned us, your majesty, when 't is remembered that the hope of Christendom lies down in danger," Sir Gerard made answer.

" 'T is a well turned speech, Sir Knight, but methinks it smacks more of court than camp. Beshrew me, the hope of Christendom, as thou dost name us, hath but a man's body with its many infirmities, and our eyes are fairly holden with sleep. I will but close one a little space while the other doth keep faithful watch 'gainst the coming of any Saracen dogs," saying which he flung him from his horse, and straight sought a grassy spot where he stretched him for slumber.

There remained naught for us save to dismount, which we did, fastening our steeds, and seating us on the ground, a little apart from the king, who lay a'ready wrapped in slumber.

I rested me 'gainst a tree. The sun burned with such mighty heat it seemed like to consume the very shadows. The king's great gerfalcon perched unhooded on the saddle of his Cyprian horse, to which 't was fastened, blinked sleepily at me, and stirred the tiny silver bells on its jesses. Over the earth a great quiet was.

Grievous is my shame that I must confess it, but I fear my eyes played traitor to my intent, and closed ere I was ware of it.

The next happening of which I had knowledge was the sound, near, and not to be denied, of fast coming horsemen, many in number. Astir in a trice, the king awakened; we were but springing to horse when the barbarian horde poured upon us, outnumbering us three to one. Scarce had we time to assume armor, the which had been put off for resting, ere we were in hand-to-hand conflict, the king, as ever, in the midst, laying about with mighty blows, which left many a cleft turban to tell the tale.

In the struggle, I being hard bestead by a Saracen emir, and having all of fighting to which I could give attendance, lost sight of my lord the king: when I again beheld him he was separate from us by the distance of some twenty paces, and was well nigh surrounded by his enemies.

In an instant of time I saw Jerusalem's hopes in the dust, England bereft of her king, and chivalry of its greatest ornament. Scarce knowing that which I would do, I spurred forward, and, dashing in the midst of his captors, said, in the lingua franca, —

"I am the king! spare my life;" and I blessed that day the mighty stature which gave color to my lie.

Swift as the thought of man, the Saracens, who even now had laid their infidel hands upon the person of the king, and were seeking to disarm him, forsook him, and fell fiercely upon me. Whilst I was being bound fast, and made prisoner in their hands, despite my struggle, the king, seeing my intent from the first, but, nathless, little liking to yield him to it, continued to lay about him with mighty blows as, if, perchance, he yet hoped to release us from our plight.

Fearing he would so enrage our enemies that they seize him also, I fell a-pleading with him in English, trusting that none other about had knowledge of this tongue.

"My lord, my lord, I beseech thee hold thy hand lest thou make my presumptuous lie vain. Flee whilst thou may, I implore thee."

"Nay, that I will not; Richard were not Plantagenet an he could thus forsake such friend as thou," quoth he hotly.

"Then hear me, your majesty. By St. George, and by every other saint, Norman or Saxon, if thou wilt not give heed to me and save thyself, an ever I am free of these my bonds again, and have use of my hands, I will on that instant draw my sword and fall thereon. If Godfrey de Bersac may not serve his king he may not live;" and this I uttered in a tone of such grim meaning that the king was not given to doubt an I meant it fully.

At this instant the rest of our knights, having despatched the body of Saracens who had set on them, came swiftly to our aid, and my captors, fearing a rescue, seized the bridle of my destrier, and I felt my steed bounding over the earth at a pace which soon lost me to sight of my comrades.

How long we rode, how much of space we compassed, I wot not, for my thoughts were of so heavy a nature that they did weigh down each moment 'til it needs must drag most wearily; but this of a surety, the sun was past the meridian, and declined toward evening ere we beheld the Saracen camp. Then did my captors slacken their pace and let the jaded steeds fall to a walk — which of a truth had become a necessity with mine own beast, it being of so heavy a build 't was hard pressed to keep abreast of the fleet Arab coursers.

When we were at length come within the camp much excitement was there, the soldiers being run together 'til they did throng us. The Sharif Taleb Ebn Amru — of whose name I came later to know and have much cause to remember — being in command of our party, did order that the soldiery disperse and go each to his own place. Howbeit, such was their joy at thought of the capture of Richard, that command and imprecation fell on deaf ears, and they so pressed upon us that at length Taleb drew his cimeter, beating back the crowd 'til he forced them let us pass to the entrance of a great silken pavilion, where I was taken from my horse and straight led within.

'Twas a spacious apartment, and all things bespoke it the dwelling of one, rich, powerful, mayhap royal. The inner walls of the tent were hung with rich silken fabric of wondrous and splendid broidering; skins of tigers and other wild beasts covered the floor, while midst a hill of soft and silken pillows half sat, half-reclined a man, clad in a loose robe of thinnest silk, heavily broidered in golden stitchery, wearing on his head a light turban stuck about with glittering jewels. Beside him two black slaves stood, wielding with the slow grace of long usage great fans, which kept the heated air in motion.

By the stature of this man, his bearing of command, his piercing black eyes, his embrowned face and curling beard, I judged me in the presence of the great Saladin. There was, beside, a look of nobility in the countenance which accorded well with the knightly deeds of this most admirable foe. Nathless, I was soon to know not Saladin, but Saphadin, his brother, who greatly resembled him, was to be my judge.

I had opportunity to observe all things which I have named to you, whilst my captor uttered in excited speech with much graceful motioning of the hands — but in a tongue unknown to me, which was doubtless Arabic — the reason for so sudden and unannounced an intrusion.

Two words of his speech were open to my understanding, — "Malec Ric;" and I saw the eye of Saphadin glow with a sudden brightening as they fell upon his ear. Quoth he, this time in the lingua franca, which I do understand indifferently well, —

"Loose his hands and unlace his armor. 'T is not meet that so great a king as Richard should stand before us, bound as a captive slave." Then, as one of the Arabs stepped forth to do his hest, he waved him aside. "Nay, by the beard of the Prophet, thou art forgetful of his rank. Richard is no less king for being captive. Do thou unharness him thyself, noble Sharif."

Thereupon, he whom after I knew as Taleb Ebn Amru stepped forward and 'gan to undo me. Loosing the pin, and opening the ventail of my helmet, there met his sight not the fair cheek and red beard of Richard, nor Richard's eyes of piercing gray, but withal mine own scarred cheek and dark locks. When the helmet was lifted from my rough dark head, which they had thought to see covered with Richard's red-gold curls, beshrew me, another time I had died of mirth at beholding their countenances. As 't was, I fear me a look of derision lay on my lips.

Ere I was ware of his intent, the Sharif, with anger, writ large in his eye, flung mine unoffending helmet to the earth, and, raising his open palm, would, had I not drawn back from his reach, have smitten me on the cheek.

"Thou dog of a Christian, thou consumer of swine's flesh, thou worshipper of idols; 't is thy father Eblis who hath taught thee to trick a true son of the Prophet. Have a care how thou dost vent thy evil mirth, or thy head will quick follow thy helmet."

"Now, by all the saints in the calendar," quoth I, with great scorn, "it needs not the aid of so mighty a person as Eblis to teach me to trick one of thy slender wit, else hadst thou not fallen with so great readiness in my poor trap. Dost think that Richard of England, the most valiant knight in Christendom, the very flower of chivalry, would stoop to beg of an infidel who follows the heathen crescent, ' Spare my life?' A child had known better."

Thereupon the Arab drew his cimeter, holding it ready to strike, while yet he stayed his hand to question me.

"By the tomb of the Prophet, thy life is forfeit if that other, 'pon whom we had a'most laid hand, was indeed ' Malec Ric.' Speak, say thine own death sentence, or, perchance, thou 'lt lie as before."

"Nay, Saracen, thy word doeth me wrong. I would not lie to save mine own poor life. Take it, I give it gladly, rejoicing yet that 't is not Richard's."

I saw the bright blade swing aloft. Scarce had I time for an Ave. I bethought me Godfrey de Bersac's hour was come, when Saphadin's voice broke on mine ear.

"Stay yet a moment, noble Taleb, ere thy rash spirit doth force thee do that which thou 'lt regret. It beseemeth me so generous a deed, though it be done to our despite, scarce merits such ill reward."

"Doth my lord Saphadin question my right to do that which I would with mine own?" the Sharif made answer, in tone of pride.

"I question not thy right, Taleb Ebn Amru; he is thy prisoner, and being such is within thy power. I but beg thee ponder well thine act before, lest thou be forced to give it too great thought when 't is past mending. 'T is said of all men that Richard's hand is ever open to requite faithful service. I doubt not he 'll e'en offer a prince's ransom for this noble knight ere he allow him suffer for his generous act. Bethink you well, 't will be a great sum, which, if thou bring down thy blade, as thou art purposed to do, will be cut off in a twinkling."

"I have sworn by the tomb of the Prophet; mine oath doth bind me, Saphadin. Stay me not from fulfilling it," quoth Taleb, in answer.

"Doth Taleb the wise forget that which the Koran doth allow? Hear ye it: 'Allah will not punish you for an inconsiderate word in your oaths: but he will punish you for what ye solemnly swear in your deliberation. And the expiation of such an oath shall be the feeding of ten poor men with such moderate food as ye feed your own families withal: or to clothe them: or to free the neck of a true believer from captivity; but he who shall not find wherewith to perform one of these things shall fast three days.'"

"Nay, then, since thou art of a mind to hear it, know that I had rather this infidel's blood flowing at my feet than any golden stream that Malec Ric could pour there. He hath tricked Taleb Ebn Amru, and hath laughed him to scorn, moreover, and for this he shall die. I have spoken," quoth he, folding his arms, as one who had made an end of a thing.

Upon this there broke from the emirs who stood around a murmur of disapproving, and I saw that only he, in whose power my life lay, desired to rend it from me.

"Then," saith Saphadin, raising him to his full height, and gazing upon mine adversary with a frown of righteous wrath, — "Then do I appeal to Allah himself. We will consult the Koran;" saying which he clapped his hands twice, and two slaves appeared in a twinkling, bearing a bowl of perfumed water and a woollen napkin.

When Saphadin had performed his ablutions, yet two other slaves came, these bearing on a broidered silken cushion a copy of the Koran, whose jewelled cover bore on it — as I did later learn to know — these words in Arabic: "Let none touch me but they who are clean."

One of the slaves bowed him forward and received the cushion and its burden on his back, having a care that the book did not sink below the level of any man's girdle — for 't is counted a grievous fault if a Moslem so hold his sacred volume.

Saphadin, drawing his cimeter, looked to heaven. "Bismillah," saith he, which in our tongue doth mean, "In the name of the living God" — thereupon he placed the point of his blade 'twixt the leaves of the book and laid it open.

"God is God, and Mohammed is his Prophet. Praise be to God for that he hath so settled our disagreement. Hear ye what the book doth pronounce.

"'Serve God and associate no creature with him; and show kindness to parents, and orphans, and the poor, and your neighbor who is kin to you, and also your neighbor who is a stranger, and your familiar companion, and the traveller, and the *captive whom your right hand shall* possess.'" When Saphadin had made an end of reading, the face of each wore a look of awe, and, verily, mine own countenance must have been likewise; for 't was as if a miracle had come betwixt me and mine adversary's hate to turn aside his sword from me.

Saphadin spake again; saith he, " 'T is thy right, noble Sharif, to take this, thy prisoner, to thine own tent, and keep him as thou art minded, until such time as he be ransomed or otherwise disposed of; but, and if it please thee allow him remain beneath the walls of my tent, I 'll e'en reward thy consideration by a present of two she-camels, great with young, and two lusty and comely female slaves. Wilt thou have it so?"

Taleb inclined his turban, making the while a move of acceptance, for he seemed yet dumb of surprise at what had befallen.

"But thou wilt make thyself answerable for him, Saphadin?"

"I swear by Him who holds my soul within his hands, that if I yield not thy captive in safety to thy keeping when the time is, that my life and all my goods are forfeit unto thee, my wives shall become thy slaves, and my slaves the slaves of thine. Is it enough?"

"It is enough," returned Taleb, and, bowing his head, passed from the tent. A motion from Saphadin's hand bade the crowd follow, and soon we were alone, save for the slaves.

'T was then he did extend to me his hand with most friendly grasping.

"I know not thy name or lineage, Sir Knight of the Cross, but thine act hath proclaimed thee noble and thy courage hath made thee kin to all brave men. I would I could have thee 'neath my tent curtains as guest, not prisoner. Thou hast heard the vow by which I bound me to deliver thee safely. If thou wilt give an oath to me that thou wilt stay as thou art, nor strive to escape so long as thou art in my keeping, it may be as I desire. Swear it, by thy Prophet, whom thou dost believe to be God, by Issa Ben Miriam. Nay, that oath may not bind thee so strongly as another. Swear, rather, if thou dost break thy word, that by this act thou dost admit that in the garden of Paradise thou shalt walk with black-eyed houris and know bodily satisfaction, — swear by this."

"Thou hast well selected thine oath, Moslem; a true Christian had rather die the death than affirm that most abhorrent belief. But thou shouldst have known, noble Saphadin, nor this oath, nor any, were needed. Think you I could peril the life and fortune of one but for whose help my head and body had ere this severed a long and close companionship. Thou hast but a mean opinion of a Christian knight."

"Thou hast spoken truth, Sir Knight; I am fairly rebuked. Thou shalt give me no oath; thine honor shall be all the chain which binds thee."

Thus abode I many weeks 'neath the tent curtains of Saphadin, ever receiving at his hands most gentle hospitality; but of a truth, when there came to mine ear tales of battles lost and battles won, in which Godfrey de Bersac bore no part; when I must needs see Saphadin ride forth with the army to war 'gainst mine own people, whilst I remained behind in the tents like a sick wench, beshrew me, the garment of courtesy was well nigh rent to rags, and must needs undergo much daily patching an it keep fit for decent cover. With any save that most generous foe it had not been possible to endure this, and my churlish temper had ceased to smoulder and 'gan to blaze.

When my lord Saphadin was within the camp, many hours we passed at chess, a game which I do play but indifferently well, and at which mine adversary did often beat me right soundly.

Withal, time pressed sorely upon me, and my thoughts were oft as heavy as the lagging day. Much I feared for Ronald, that since my captivity some ill might have befallen him, though I scarce had been able to put into words what evil I dreaded. Of a certainty I knew

Richard would not be unmindful of the boy, knowing how I loved him, and despite that John o' Bardon, my other squire, had ever held himself jealously toward the child, yet I was not for fearing he would do aught to serve him ill. Nathless, ofttimes in the deep of night, when slumber locked my sense, I would have heavy dreams of the boy who ever wore in my visions the sorrowful look he had wistful turned toward me as I rode from camp on the day of my capture. Sometimes, in my imagining, he seemed astray on the desert, alone, perishing for water, and calling upon me to come to his aid; always some ill threatened him.

On a day, some weeks of my coming to the Saracen camp, my lord Saphadin and I played at chess. I had, because of the heat and my enforced sloth, taken upon me to wear the thin silken garments in which the Saracens were wont to array themselves. Thus habited, we reclined 'mongst soft cushions, the hot air being fanned to continuous motion by the slaves, this giving something of comfort to our heated bodies.

The Saracen had but now mated my king for the third time of the morn, and I, in churlish displeasure at being thus beaten, had brushed the pieces into an heap and remained staring sourly at them.

"Now by the beard of the Prophet, Sir Knight, thou shouldst not bear me ill-will for this small defeat, seeing that but yestermorn our army must needs take a far heavier one at the hands of thy soldiery."

At which saying, my brows came together still more blackly, for his words were as a goad to my fretted spirit.

"Of a truth 't is well said, but what part or lot hath Godfrey de Bersac in such victory, reclining here in soft luxury like a sick wench?" I made churlish demand.

Quick there leaped to his countenance a look which gave me to know that my rough tongue had inflicted hurt on mine enemy who was come to be so greatly my friend.

"Surely thou art ware, Godfrey," saith he in tone which held an understanding sorrow in its depth, "an thou wert my prisoner only, I had long ere this sent thee back to Richard, without awaiting a paltry ransom. Such an act as thine deserves so much of recognition from all brave men; beside this, I like not to behold day by day the restless fretting of a snared lion."

At the which my sorry mood passed shamefacedly from me.

"I cry thee pardon, Saphadin. Thou art ever the most generous of foes, and I bethink me 't is but poor return I make to thee for thy many favors, with my sour tempers and peevish frettings. I take shame to myself because of them." Whereupon mine adversary, smiling, 'gan to right the overturned board and set his pieces in order for another battle.

With an impatient shaking of my huge body I withdrew from my reclining posture and stood upright.

"Nay, nay, my lord, no more of chess to-day, I beg. Thou hast the brains of me in the game, and I am for letting well alone that which I do so ill," saying which I passed to the opening of the tent — for a shouting and unwonted commotion without had caught my hearing. At a distance I beheld many Saracen soldiers run together, there appearing to be something unaccustomed going forward 'mongst them, for great turmoil prevailed.

I clapped my hands three times, and straight there appeared before me, as he had sprung from the earth beneath my feet, the black slave, who, by Saphadin's order, attended on my special bidding.

Pointing to the group, I bade him run quickly, see what was going forward, and bring me word. Ere the command was fairly from my mouth he had sped on the way, and was returned a'most before I knew him gone. Not 'til he had knelt at my feet again, and pressed the earth with his forefront, would he deliver himself of his errand. For 't is the way of these black slaves to crouch in an humbleness to which a well-born English hound would scarce demean himself. Nor would he ever address me save in titles of exaggerated honor, "most worshipful," "great white king of the earth," and many more such, that my memory holds no longer. I dare be sworn it had never pierced his black skull that I was not indeed the wonderful Malec Ric, of whose prowess he had doubtless heard such tales as to deem him little short of a god.

"Most majestic and gracious one, 't is said that the soldiers have captured a young Frankish lad spying near the camp, and have fetched him within; that, moreover, the youth is well nigh perished for lack of food and water."

I turned toward Saphadin, whose quick understanding read my wish. "Go bid them bring the prisoner before me without delay," he commanded the slave.

In a short space of time I saw the crowd surge toward our tent, surrounding the lad, who was half led, half borne in their midst. When they were come anear, my eager gaze discerned the face of Ronald; thin, 'til the skull of him lay open to view 'neath the drawn skin of his face; white with the whiteness of death, the lips blue and swollen, unkempt, miserable and footsore, yet, withal, Ronald. Upon seeing me he gathered strength to break from his captors. Uttering a mighty cry of joyfulness, he fell at my feet. "Master, master, master!" saith he, when I had raised him pitifully and held him 'gainst my arm, the which he kept smoothing over with his weak hands and pressing gently, as though he feared me unreal.

"Ronald, what doest thou here," I made stern demand, for on the sight of him I came nigh to guessing the reason of his presence.

He gave a weak laugh, nor seemed to heed my question, his fingers continuing to stray over my arm and body. "Thou art real, thou art not but a shadow of my crazed brain; I have found thee at length?" saith he, and so saying his brown eyes closed and his sense fled him.

"My lord," quoth I, turning to Saphadin, who looked wonderingly upon us, "I pray you bid these men begone about their affairs. This is no spy, but mine own squire, who, unless I mistake not, hath stolen from Richard's camp in search of me, for whom he doth bear a foolish love;" and without further ado, nor waiting leave of any, I raised the boy in my arms and bore him to my own tent a-joining, where I placed him on my pallet, and 'gan to lave his face with cold water, 'til his sense was come to him again.

I heard not a little of murmuring 'mongst those without who had taken the lad, and some complaining at being thus deprived of their prisoner, and 't was not 'til Saphadin's voice had sounded several times in sharp command that the complaining died away and the crowd dispersed.

When Ronald had unclosed his eyes again,

feeling the cool bath upon his face, he was for a little as one possessed at sound of the falling water. With feeble motions of his hands he strove to make me see his want; and when I did not, being strangely lackbrained, he gathered enough of strength to raise himself and seize the ewer from my hand. Turning it to his mouth he drank and drank, giving forth little sounds of satisfaction the while, 'til I, fearing the boy would harm himself with so heavy a draught after long thirst, strove with him, at length gaining the ewer from his tight clasped hands.

When he lay back on the couch once more, 't was some space of time ere he would give heed to my questioning, or seem to hear me, he being minded to lie with a great look of content in his hollow eyes, and gaze on me as he feared, an he so much as move, I would slip from his vision on the instant and be resolved into thin air.

"Master, master, master!" saith he again, and yet again, in such varying tone that his one poor word did seem to sum and hold all other love speech in it.

Howbeit, after a time I coaxed him to his wit, and bade him word his tale to me and say why I found him thus, half dead within the Saracen camp.

"Chide me not, my lord, for that I could not live absent from thee," he did humbly plead, his great eyes brimming with love still fixed on me. "After thou wert made captive, my heart was well-nigh breaking, despite that all had care and kindness toward me. When days passed into weeks, and still I saw thee not, or knew aught of thy fate, my feeling brake all bonds. On a night I stole John o' Bardon's horse, Mohammed being lame of leg, and crept from the camp when darkness and sleep covered all. I knew not which way to turn an I go toward thee, but I prayed to the blessed Mother of God to have guidance of me, and rode on and on I knew not whither. When day was come, after a long dark night wherein black shadows seemed ever about to start into an army of villain Turks ready to seize and rend me, I saw that I was lost to sight of our camp, nor beheld I any other in which thou mightest be. I had fetched with me but little food, and a small skin of water, having come to sudden resolve to seek thee while I tossed sleepless on my pallet. When I sought food, to bear with me on this journey, I found little in the larder, and I could not, of my impatience, wait the coming and going of another day ere I departed.

"All day I rode while the sun burned hot on us and thirst 'gan shortly to rage. I shared the water with the poor horse who suffered greatly, but the little that I could give him seemed to scarce more than wet his muzzle. Nathless, I had good hope soon to find thee, and, it being the time for rains to fall, I scanned the sky for a cloud, thinking that at any moment relief might so be brought to us. All day the sky was as a cover of burnished brass, nor bush nor tree gave ever so little of shadow wherein we might cool ourselves. Night came on: the chill of it entered my very bones causing me to become sore and heavy. I lay down beside the horse, striving to sleep, but fear was on me and I could not. I drew as close as I might to the beast, thrusting my arm across his neck, for that, being alive, he seemed to yield me comfort in that awful loneliness in which I 'gan to doubt if I were not the only living being left upon the earth. The dew fell so heavily and my thirst was now become so great that I essayed to draw a little of moisture from the sleeve of my surcoat; but 'twas scarce wet enough for this though it had the feel as of my having been drawn from a stream.

"Day broke and the sun came up and warmed my chilled bones to burning heat, and yet no water could I find though I searched diligently: and still the heavens were locked up 'gainst our awful need. Step by step the way was become more barren, 'til, gaze which way I might, only hot, dry sands stretched before me. When night was fallen again I think my wit 'gan to go from me, for I did seem to spy cool running streams, which no sooner having come upon and stooping to quaff of, than straightly they would vanish into the earth and my lips meet naught but burning sand. Then thou wouldst appear before me, my lord, and when I strove to clasp and hold thee, thou wouldst turn to thin air and be gone like a spirit.

"Another day broke, and well-nigh powerless now for lack of food I wandered on for a time 'til the horse at length refused to stir, but stood with nose to the earth and drooping ears, nor heeded my feeble effort when I strove to move him by force. Already were the great dark birds of prey circling and circling above, marking him where he stood nor doubting that he would shortly fill their hungry maws. An it had not been for fear of these, of their sharp beaks and yet sharper talons rending my poor body, perchance ere life had fled, I had then and there laid me down beside the beast and let go my little hold of life. Howbeit I pressed on weakly, thy face ever rising before me an I stumble or lose my footing, and when I was for deeming it no longer possible to move, that I must needs lie there in the hot sand and die, thy voice would sound in mine ear 'Up, Ronald, up,' and, striving as ever to obey thy commands, I would once more press on 'til strength did again forsake me. Thus it was throughout all that day; when, just before the fall of darkness mine eyes beheld this hill in the distance and the gleam of tents thereon.

'Twas long ere I knew an it were real, and not mine own witless dreaming shadowed forth as a vision. I hid myself and waited 'til the darkness fell and time for sleep was come; then I crept softly anear the camp, and, by fortune, chanced upon a sentry who slept at his post. His sleep being right heavy I was enabled to steal from his neck the water skin which by the blessing of the saints had still enough of water within its depths to yield me a joy-giving draught. Drinking, I crept 'mongst the rocks and hid and slept 'til the break of day. When I awoke, I knew not what to do. I feared to go within the camp lest I be taken captive and thou not there: nathless, I was ware an I did not, another day was like to see my spirit sped with hunger and thirst. The while I skulked about trying to find somewhat upon which to stay my stomach, a Turk fell on me unawares and haled me hence. Now, thanks be to the blessed Virgin, I am with thee; and if thou wilt have it so, I would mightily relish somewhat to eat, for it hath been nigh on to three days since I tasted food or water save for the drop I stole from the sleeping Turk yesternight."

After Ronald's coming the days hung not so wearily upon me. The lad was himself within a week's time and his presence did not a little to lighten my moods. From him I learned of all the happenings to the army of the cross since my leading into captivity: of the despatches which were come from England telling Richard of the evil doing of his brother John, who was like to rend the throne from him an the king came not soon to claim his own. And how, after much sorrow of mind, Richard had at length proclaimed to the army, that despite the great need of his return to England, he would nathless remain in the Holy Land 'til after Easter. All this and much beside he unfolded to me,. and long hours we talked of battles won and battles lost; but and if our speech turned, as it was sometimes like, to England or our going thither, straight fell a cloud on Ronald's face, he seeming no longer to hold interest in aught.

At all other times, howbeit, he were as blithe and gay as he were the freest, richest knight in all Christendom, and not poor squire, serving a poor master, captive 'mongst infidels, nor knowing from whence his ransom would come or indeed if he would have any. Ofttimes the boy warbled prettily to himself and sometimes did enliven our dulness by striving to execute a ballad or a love lay upon the barbarous instruments that the Turks do use from which to draw music withal. And did he word or did he play, 'twas ever the same; content filled his brown eyes and laughter lay not far from his red mouth.

My memory doth love to linger over these days, which though I had little thought on it then, were so soon drawing to a sorry end. I bear small doubt of who brought that grievous end to pass, despite that proof 'gainst the villain was never brought to light: but it doth warm the cockles of my heart to call to mind that in after time he came to pay in full the price of his evil toward Ronald. Mine eyes had not been closed to the ill feeling which mine enemy, Taleb Ebn Amru, still bore toward me, for though he refrained himself from doing aught, he ever cast black looks upon me an he pass me in the way.

But to my tale once more, for thou hast as yet no knowledge of these happenings of which I prate.

'Twas the nightly custom, by my Lord Saphadin's order, since my dwelling within the Saracen camp, that the slaves set beside my pallet a flagon of wine, from which I took a good draught ere I lay down to slumber. In this Saphadin showed himself a most gentle host, for, being a follower of Mohammed, and zealous in this infidel belief, he took no wine or fermented drink himself; nathless he had thought to my Norman thirst, which, though not large, is most compelling.

It fell out on the night of which I would speak that, being monstrously thirsty, I had swallowed a well-filled stoup of the wine set for me, and had poured a lesser potion for Ronald, which 'twas his nightly wont to take ere leaving my tent for his own, near by.

"'T is poor stuff, Ronald," quoth I, holding the vessel toward him; for now that the liquor was on the inside of me, I was ware that it had a taste passing strange for good wine. "These infidels have great knowledge on some points, but naught of good wine, beshrew me."

Ronald tasted the potion; twisting his face wryly, he set it down.

"By St. Hilary, the stuff hath a right bitter flavor, and I like it not," quoth he; and he wished me gentle slumber and passed from the tent, leaving the wine untouched.

Oft have I in bitterness of spirit harked back to that hour, wishing that the lad had taken his potion and slept his drugged sleep, as he was most like to have done, for then, mayhap, he might be with me now; but straight on the footsteps of this wish I see so much of after knowledge crowd, I doubt not that 'twas for the best that all happened as it did. Ronald's going held less of pain to him, I trow, than his staying would have brought.

From now must I word thee the tale of this event as I after gathered it through the broken utterance of Ronald and the speech of the frightened slaves: for from the hour I fell on slumber that night, after swallowing the stoup of wine, I knew naught of what went forward 'til mine eyes unclosed heavily, and with great unwillingness, upon a frightened group of slaves about my couch, together with Saphadin himself, who held within his arms, Ronald, wounded and well-nigh dead.

'T is said that in the deep of the night, Ronald awoke from a light slumber. The sound of stealthy movement in my tent caught his quick ear. At first he deemed it but a trick of his half-dreaming brain, and had straightly turned to slumber again an a louder sound of something falling had not brought him to broad wakefulness. Creeping from his couch then, he softly pushed aside my tent curtains, and in the dim blackness faintly descried figures moving near my couch. Uttering a frighted cry, he sprang forward and threw a tight clasp about the body of a man, to whom he clung with a fierce grip, crying out the while to arouse the sleeping slaves. Despite that the villain strove with all his force to loose himself from the boy's grasp, he clung to him doughtily. Again and yet again did Ronald's cry sound out, 'til at length the slaves were wakened and came running with lights. Saphadin came also, knowing not what had on a sudden befallen. Howbeit, ere these were arrived, the villain with whom Ronald grappled, had loosed himself, having smote the lad with a knife, leaving two deep wounds in the body of him, from which his life blood poured.

Through all of this I had been in heavy sleep beside my pallet, from which I had been dragged and bound fast, hand and foot; while my mouth was wrapped firmly about with a silken scarf, so that in case of my waking I had not been able to make outcry. The tent wall showed a long clean-cut rift, through which the villains had admitted themselves and through which they had doubtless purposed to bear me; to what fate I know not, save only this, an Taleb Ebn Amru had the naming of it, beshrew me. I like not to dwell upon the thought, even now, though I be nothing cowardly.

Ronald, despite his wounds, had crawled to my side while the slaves unbound me and strove to waken me from my heavy slumbers. But mine eyes were so fast holden with sleep that I knew naught until after long shaking. Through all this time the boy hung over me, crying and calling heaven to witness that I was a'ready dead, and refusing comfort of any. At length when mine eyes were come apart, my dazed sense strove slowly in me. I beheld the boy's white face close to mine own, and felt his tears warm upon my hand; while around us stood the staring crowd of slaves and torch-bearers; fright marking every countenance for thinking if perchance blame might not fall heavily on them for this night's work.

I raised myself heavily, questioning of what all meant, whereupon, ere any could heed or answer, I saw Roland slip aside and fall, losing his sense.

'T was long ere my clouded mind could grasp these happenings, for the drug still worked within me. Saphadin had of his pitifulness removed Ronald, and Saladin's own leech was come quickly to attend upon him, ere I was in my proper mind again: but 't was of little avail, for the knife had dealt death at each stroke, and 't was but a matter of hours now ere the boy's spirit be sped. When the leech at length gave place to me beside Ronald's couch I saw that he did cast strange looks upon me, but never dreamed I their import until later, when Ronald had unfolded his pitiful tale to my hearing.

As I bent beside the boy I saw that the grey shadows of death were fast eating up the fair roundness of his face, but in his eyes there dwelt a look that held the glory of heaven. Though I be man it shamed me not that mine own eyes were become fountains of salt water as I gazed on the untimely ending of one so fitted for life. I essayed speech, but my tongue clove to the roof of my mouth and no sound could I utter.

"Grieve not thus, Godfrey," saith he, seeing this and reaching forth a weak hand to touch my face. "I have much to tell thee, which having heard, thou'lt then be assured that my passing is for my happiness. The saints have been good to me in this, for my death hath served to rescue my kingdom and my king; for thou art both of these."

Then 'gan he to word a tale so passing strange, I had fain thought him raving an he spake not so calmly. And by this tale I was ware that 't was no lad who had shared my poor fare, served me as henchman, fought and marched at my side, bearing our hard life with so brave a face that I was e'en rejoiced to think, when his age was ripe therefor, I myself would lay the accolade on his shoulder.

What boots her pitiful tale of lament and rebellion that she was born a wench in a family of wenches; her dreams of glory, her longings which did break forth to action, fired by unceasing talk of the Crusades.

"The blood of a soldier beat in my veins, Godfrey, the heart of a soldier throbbed 'neath my wimple. On a night as I lay tossing on my couch, I resolved to go to Palestine, wench or no. Then donned I man's attire, and as well as I might I donned his courage also. Alas I wist not what it was to be a man; the perils I feared not, but the hardships burdened my woman's flesh, all unused to aught save dainty fare and soft housing. I dared not turn back, I scarce dared press forward. At Vezelai, where I was come after much toil, I joined me to the knight Ranulf de Roveirie and fared as best I might 'mongst his rough troopers.

"Thou knowest of our meeting at Messina, and from thenceforward my tale is thine also. Of all thy gentleness to me since, how can I speak my gratefulness—" but here I stopped her prating, for well thou art ware, rough Godfrey de Bersac knows naught of gentleness.

So amazed was I at her words that I wist not what to say. As my little comrade I had been ready enough of speech with her, but the simple knowledge that she was not man like myself, seemed on the instant to bear her far from me, leaving me abashed and silent. Already were past events thronging before me, mine eyes opened now to a new sad understanding of them. A pain, the like of which, God be thanked, has never fallen on me again, was now gripping my heart; the pain which comes of knowledge of another, wounded, perchance mortally, at thy hand, despite that it was unwitting done.

"I would that I had lived to take the order of knighthood at thy hands and to aid a little longer in this righteous cause in which we war, but God hath not so ordered it and I rest content in having served thee," saith she when she had gathered strength to speak again.

"Thou shalt not go hence, comrade, lacking one boon which thou dost crave; for though thou art not to wear thy spurs in this world, who can say thou 'lt not pass to another where good fighting is, and where thy knighthood will avail thee something. Rise Sir Ronald de Glanville, true knight and valiant soldier," and I did touch her soft three times upon the shoulder with my blade.

Then flashed a look of great joy within her eyes and while I held aloft before her steady gaze the cross upon my sword hilt, she breathed forth the vow of knighthood, which bound her to gentle deeds, the upholding of the innocent, and the succor of the weak. After which a silence fell for a long minute, and when she spake again her voice was changed and faltering.

"When, or if thou shalt return to England," she paused, then pressed on bravely, "seek out my father if he be yet alive; relate to him my wanderings. Tell him of my end and where my body lies. Say to him though I but ill played the man, I yet did naught which misbecame my womanhood. That be all — now fetch hither the priest that I may make my peace with God;" for, thanks be to the saints, there was a holy father 'mongst the prisoners in the camp, and Ronald needs not to go unhousled to the grave.

So heavy was I with sorrow at all to which I had given ear, that I stumbling sought my feet to do her bidding. As I was passing from the tent, she uttered my name in voice so weak I scarce could catch the sound thereof, yet withal, 'twas fraught with a something new to mine ear. I turned me about and met a look from her eyes, a look such as page gives not to master, nor comrade to comrade. Untutored as I was, I yet understood, and hastened to her. I was not unmindful of my love, my lady, nor deemed I myself unfaithful for that I raised the dying child in my arms and laid a long and tender kiss upon her mouth.

When I lifted my head, the flush on her face well-nigh chased from it the shadows of death. My heart was moved to such pity and yearning, that words of endearment rushed to my lips; ere I could give utterance to them she stayed me with her soft hand on my lips.

"Nay, Godfrey, say no word. I know full well that all thy great and loyal heart is in another's keeping. Thou lovest her, even as I love thee. I have no shame to say it, — as I love thee," and she did utter each word with such dwelling tenderness as wrung my heart to self-hatred. "Some day — some time, long hence — thou wilt tell her of this. Say to her — beloved — beloved — nay, I cannot tell it thee — thou wilt know how to word it for me." She paused, and turning her face hid it for a time on my breast. I held her tenderly, my lips laying soft kisses on her fair curls, my tongue palsied from sorrow. "Now of thy goodness go, and send the holy father," she murmured at length and lay back from my arms spent and weak.

I went, walking as one being sightless, all things dancing before me in a haze.

'T was long ere the priest summoned me again to her side and unconsciousness was fallen on her sense; she knowing me not nor seeming other than dead save for a faint and labored breathing.

I have faced death full many times on the field of battle but never seemed he so grim as in those hours when he did sit face to face with me over against the body of the lad I loved so well. For to me she was still but a lad and my gallant little comrade, save when the memory of that kiss rose up to deny her manhood.

The far sounds of the early morning camp, cries, oaths, and laughter 'gan now to press hard on the near silence about us, as there were no place in the busy world for the quiet of death.

I rose and pushed aside the tent curtain. The rising sun sent a long ray across the earth 'til it rested like a flame on the child's face, glorifying it beyond measure. Her eyes unclosed; "Beloved," she whispered, smiling with soft content as one who greets her love, with now no thought of parting; and on the instant her spirit sped.

Of the mad sorrow which raged in my heart after Ronald's passing I have no word to tell thee. My thoughts lived over each event of our common life, I striving ever to see wherein I might have guarded her 'gainst this sorrowful end; naming myself the while a doting fool in that I had not sooner read her piteous secret.

But did regret for the child's loss bear heavily upon me, swift on its footsteps pressed the knowledge that she had not brooked to live and have me return to Weregrave, to my love. Beshrew me, I am no cockloach,[1] but there was that in Ronald's eyes which gave me to doubt if time or circumstance could lightly turn her heart from me to another; and great shame seized upon me for that I blamed myself, that her love had been thus given me, though to this hour I scarce can see wherein doth lie my fault.

On the morrow, Ronald was borne to her grave, it being on the crest of the hill; for I would that she lay as near by to heaven as we could raise her. Over the place of her burying I bade the slaves raise an heap of stones so that no prowling beast could ere disturb her slumbers.

Saphadin spared not the use of the rod 'mongst the slaves of his household, trusting thereby to gain some knowledge of how the sleeping potion was come in my wine flagon. Howbeit, naught could we discover from the howling blackamoors, who one and all swore by Allah and the Prophet that they had borne no hand therein. Despite this fact, 'twas more than guessed betwixt us that in some way it had been the foul work of Taleb Ebn Amru — who had purposed to bear

[1] Silly cockscomb.

me away and take vengeance of his hatred upon me, the while he claimed that I had fled of myself, and in so doing forfeited Saphadin's wives and goods and slaves to him. 'Twas a well-laid plan, and had not poor Ronald awakened as he did, great sorrow had fallen on all of us because of it.

Of the days which followed Ronald's death, there is little to recount, for my spirit bore itself so heavily, I scarce observed their passing. The long confinement within the camp told greatly on my bodily health and my face looked back on me from the polished metal mirror as pale as any wench's.

Then was the dulness of life a little lightened for me by the breaking of camp, I being fetched to the new camp which lay well concealed within the hills scarce nine leagues[1] distant from Joppa. From the highest point of the hill on which we lay, my longing eyes could see in the valley on the north side of the distant city, the tents of the Christian army. Day by day I climbed to the spot — for by Saphadin's orders I was let to have all freedom possible — and here would I watch the distant specks which marked the place where mine own people were. Much I pondered of the cause of the long delay in the coming of my ransom; ofttimes even doubting if perchance Godfrey de Bersac's name were any longer held in remembrance of any.

[1] In the Middle Ages a league was about two miles.

On a day as I came thence from my vigil, I turned aside out of my path, casting myself down amongst the rocks in weariness of all that the earth held. My thoughts were dwelling sorrowfully upon Ronald in the lone grave near the sky, and of the child's exceeding great love for me which I had so ill deserved. From this sore matter they passed at length to my fair love in distant England, who I doubted not was even then awaiting my return. While I lay thus, with face upturned to the sky I 'gan to dream of that hour of home-coming and to shadow it forth in my mind as a real thing. I pictured how first I should behold my lady, and what words she would have in greeting for me: I saw her again standing tall and fair, backed by the dull grey stones of Weregrave, while within her eyes burned the look which they had worn on the day I parted from her. Musing thus of love, there sudden fell on my startled ear, the sound of a voice so near, 'twas as if one spake from directly beneath me. I sprung to a sitting posture nothing doubting, that from behind some rock or bush I should see the saucy face of Robin Goodfellow himself, come hither from distant England to play his prankish tricks upon us still. Had it been so, I had then and there given the pucksy sprite a warmer welcome than he was wont to get of mortals; for I was in the mood to love even a devil, if only he be a good Norman devil from over seas, and wear a straight English tongue in his head.

No spirit or devil caught my roving gaze, howbeit, and I was for thinking mine ears had tricked me, when I spied a crevice in the rock beneath me which seemed to run deep below the surface. While mine eyes fastened themselves on this, wondering if perchance it had aught to do with this strange happening, I again heard the voice, which seemed of a certainty to reach me through the rock rift. This time my hatred gave my hearing to know that 't was the tongue of mine enemy that spake.

Saith the voice of Taleb Ebn Amru, for 't was he, though where he was I knew not: " The sun declines."

Then a voice whose sound was unfamiliar to my hearing, made answer.

" Aye, but another and brighter shall rise."

To which mine enemy returned, " May it rise quickly and shine brightly."

" Amen to that say I," quoth the other.

" Thou art bearer of word to me from the great lord Conrad of Montserrat, unless I mistake," quoth Taleb Ebn Amru, dropping on a sudden his light tone for one of more serious import.

Upon hearing the name of the Marquis of Montserrat, whom Richard greatly mistrusted, if camp tales were not untrue — he deeming him scarce more than a runagate knave — I listened yet more closely, hesitating not to place mine ear 'gainst the rock rift, which having done I then heard all speech that passed betwixt these two as I had been on the spot.

"If thou art the Emir Taleb Ebn Amru, as I judge thou art from thy answers to my speech, thou art right in thinking me the bearer of word to thee. Conrad of Montserrat bade me hither to meet thee at this place and give to thy hand this parchment, it being the signed agreement which thou didst demand of him."

After a short space of time, in which I doubt not the Emir took cognizance of the content of the parchment, for I could even hear it crackle 'neath his touch, I heard him again hold speech with the messenger. 'Twas then he unfolded a tale of such twofold treachery that it did make my blood boil and surge only to listen thereto, and not straightly be able to smite the schemers.

This was the word which the false Emir sent to the false Marquis,— namely, that all was in readiness for the stroke, and even this night, Saladin and Saphadin both being absent and the Emir in command, it was purposed that a large band of Saracens would ride from the camp. These would come quietly and with great caution on the Christians in the gray dawn, ere the hour of waking. But before this general attack was made, it was designed that three of the bravest of the soldiers should steal within Richard's tent and put him to death. There upon the infidel host would fall on the sleeping army, who, having no time to arm or prepare, would of a certainty be cut to pieces.

Then he further unfolded his plans and by these I knew that this treachery was of double nature, in that the Emir aspired to overthrow Saladin as well as Richard.

'Twas purposed that when the victorious Saracens returned to camp, bearing the trophy of Richard's head — confusion upon them for even such a thought — that certain of the leaders should proclaim Taleb Ebn Amru, Soldan, and there being many of the troops dissatisfied at the long-continued bloody conflict with the English, it was thought that these would join with them in the matter. So that when Saladin and Saphadin were returned to camp, 't would be to find themselves in the midst of a hostile force who were like to show scant mercy toward them.

And this be not the whole of the matter yet, for it was further designed that after Richard's murder, Conrad of Montserrat would straightly put himself at the head of the remnant of the Christian forces, and thus by the combined treachery of these two, the leaders of both forces would be in position to make a truce of great advantage to themselves, if perchance, not strictly to the liking of others.

All this I overheard with mine ear fast fixed to the rift in the rock, and while I listened I pondered of the means which lay to my hand wherewith to overthrow this scheming and save both Richard and Saladin.

The conference having come to an end, the voices ceased and I heard after a time footsteps as of some one departing, and anon the coming feet of the Saracen Emir. I thanked the saints that my place of hiding was well shut from the view of any on the path up which this treacherous dog was like to come on his return to camp; for had he glimpsed me there, or had reason for thinking me within the knowledge of his scheming, he had not spared to send me to another world by the shortest road there may be.

I therefore rested quiet 'til I heard his step come and pass, and mine ear told me that he must be safely gone from sight these many minutes. Without delay then, for an I do aught I must do it quickly, I took the path which the Emir had just now trod, being greatly desirous of finding the mystery of the rift in the rock and the greater mystery of how the messenger of Conrad was come unseen to within the guard of the Saracen camp.

Down the path I trod slowly, searching diligently for any sign of way or opening toward the direction from which I judged the voices to have come. Twice I passed over this path even down to where the sentinel paced his slow way, and no sign could I discern of any mode of egress. For be it known to you that for a matter of ten paces on one side of this path, the earth was rough and boulder strewn, and beyond this, for a great distance down the hill, ran an unbroken wall of rock to twice the height of a tall man. Nathless, 'twas from this way that the voices sounded, and only from this way could the messenger have approached unseen into the camp.

I was passing over this ground for the second time and about to give over the search which seemed like to prove fruitless and turn my thought to the pressing matter of mine own action. Belike it was that the rock rift over which I had rested had no connection with any other spot, and the voices that I had heard as by a miracle, had been borne to me from I know not where, so that by the will of God I might overthrow His enemies. Having reached this conclusion I turned about with the intent to go straightly to my tent, when mine eye was caught and held by a scrap of bright silk swinging from the point of a brier which grew over against the wall of rock. My heart bounded within me, for it was of the hue of the sash which I had beheld but this morn, bound about the middle of the Emir. I paused not long to consider that he must have lately brushed near by the bush. Clambering over the rough way, I stood close to the spot striving to see from whence he had come to this point. No path nor opening showed itself nor up nor down, only the unbroken wall and the rock-strewn earth.

Enraged and disappointed beyond measure at thus failing, I was again turning toward camp, when my impatient foot stirred a tiny pebble, which quickly rolled away and was lost to sight 'neath the dense growth of brier against the rock. On the instant, I heard it drop as from a little height. Quick as I can word it I thrust my hands amidst the briers and tore them aside. There before my wondering gaze lay an opening in the rock's side which would admit the body of a man an he double himself well together in the passing.

Enough of light was there to be ware that the bottom of the cavern was distant but a little way from the level on which I stood. I therefore drew my baselard and made ready to pass through the hole, wondering if perchance I might not encounter some ambushed enemy.

Once within, and I dare be sworn 'twas a closer squeeze for me than my Saracen enemy, I found myself able to stand upright in a spacious cavern into which a dim light filtered from a direction over against where I stood.

Pausing 'til my sight was come accustomed to the dimness, I surveyed the spot. On the earth at one side of this rockribbed cave, I faintly discerned the crouching forms of two men, who I judged from their posture to be locked in sound slumber. An instant only I took to consider my course. Should I go forward softly to see whither the cave led, trusting not to arouse mine enemies' sleep, or should I creep upon them unawares and slay them ere they wakened? I made haste to settle on this last, though my gorge rose 'gainst slaying any thus, it seeming an unknightly act. Nathless it were well to bear in mind that I, single-handed and alone, fought for a great stake, even the king's life, and that, too, 'gainst enemies who knew little of knightly scruple. So, with cautious step I advanced noiselessly upon the sleeping guards, my heart sounding in my breast 'til each instant I feared it would waken the sleepers. When near, I straightened myself, and giving a mighty thrust I plunged my baselard deep into the nearest fellow's body, only to find, when I strove to withdraw it, that the man unfolded and came apart, — that what in the dimness I had mistaken for a sleeping man was indeed but a pile of half rotted sheep skins.

Drawing a mighty breath of relief, I kicked them open, satisfying myself beyond doubt that none lay in hiding beneath. I perceived also some worn water skins and cooking pots on the ground near by which I judged the cave to have been at one time the hiding-place of some villain band of robbers such as infest the land and take unwilling tribute of peaceful inhabitants.

Turning now in haste, I followed the light for some distance, stepping carefully, lest there be any hidden pitfalls set for the unwary. I came at length to the other opening of the cavern which gave upon a steep path roughly hewn in the side of the rock, which path led to the foot of the hill, losing itself in a deep gorge betwixt this hill and the one over against it.

Now was I ware of how the messenger of the Marquis of Montserrat had come, and thus I determined under the cover of night to go. For go I must, despite my word to Saphadin, despite his pledge for me; for the life of my king lay within my hand. But and if the Lord so will and no harm befall me in the going, I would be able to reach the Christian camp, warn them of the threatened treachery, and, procuring a horse, return hither in the early morn. Had Saphadin or Saladin been within the camp I had unfolded to them this tale of double treachery, trusting to them to prevent the foul murder of such an enemy as Richard: but they both being abroad and not like to return for many days, and if Taleb Ebn Amru's plan miscarry not, they were most like to fall on treachery themselves an they did return.

Thus ran my thoughts as I retraced my steps through the cave, and made my way through the small opening again into the light — having a care when I had passed that the bush fell well into place and concealed the way of my coming, and that I had left no tell-tale shred on the briers to give my secret to the keeping of other.

Once within my tent, I 'gan on the instant to lay such plans of action as I was able, — which plans I did faithfully carry out in all particulars, as thou shalt hear later on. Having done all that I might in preparation, I threw myself upon my couch in hopes to gain a little sleep gainst my night of wakefulness and struggle. But of a truth, this I could not for fretting impatience. Never saw I the sun so long in its decline, and darkness seemed never like to fall over the earth again; nathless, in looking back on all this, I doubt not that the sun went to rest as ever, and that night fell with its wonted quickness.

When it had at length come, I sought my couch as early as might be, having a care lest I arouse suspicion of any. It was a matter of urgency that I quit the Saracen camp as soon as might be, seeing I had a'most nine leagues to make afoot whilst mine enemies, though they make a later start, would be well mounted on fleet coursers.

I deemed it most inexpedient that I go armed, or in my wonted habit for many reasons, the first of which being the weight of my shirt of mail which would greatly hinder me in the race set before me. Besides 'twere easier to pass unnoticed through the camp an I wear the disguise of a Saracen. So it was that when the sound of the heavy breathing of the two slaves who lay at my tent opening, gave me to know that quiet was over all, I hastily rose from my couch and attired me in a heathen garment of striped wool and bound about my middle a sash of yellow into which I thrust my baselard and mine own good Norman blade, trusting that in the dark none would have notice for so slight a matter as that I wore not a cimeter.

Staining my face with a brown cordial which Saphadin's leech had left for my taking — and which I promise you I had naught to do with, having small liking for brews of whatsoever sort. Howbeit, the stuff made not so bad a pigment wherewith to turn me to a superstitious infidel, save that it was villainous sticky and did dry on my skin as a plaster. Over my head I cast an Arab keffieh, which is a head covering not so large, but bearing a great resemblance to the coverchief which ladies do wear in England, save that it fastens to the head with a band of soft camels' hair rope bound over it. The ends of this covering I drew well together about the lower part of my face, concealing thus my chin, shaven clean as it was of all hair. When all this was accomplished, I loosened the tent curtain and stepped with great caution over the sleeping slaves, who stirred not nor moved at my passing. Once without the tent, 't was plain to be seen that the camp had not gone to rest, and that somewhat of an unusual nature was going forward. I walked with as much of unconcern as might be, having a care not to appear in any haste lest I call notice upon myself. My legs did fairly jump to be off in a hot run, and 't was all that my strength could, to hold them from such rash act.

I met not a few soldiers passing hither and yon who gave small heed to me, doubtless taking me for one of their own sort, which not a little quieted the pounding of my heart and brought confidence to me.

Thus I was footing it as fleetly as I dared, when, on a sudden, sounded clear through the still night air, the Muedhdhin's last call to prayer. For the instant I wot not what to do, then, quick as thought, I faced toward Mecca as I had on occasions seen these infidels do. I fell on my knees, and having first performed my ablutions in the dust, as it is permitted to the followers of Mohammet when water is not at hand, I bowed my head to the earth, and though I offered no good Mohammedan prayer, nor did I ask the intervention of the Prophet; I did of a truth beg the mother of God that she give wings to my heels this night, the while she keep a wary eye on this same meddlesome Prophet that he get not his fingers in my affairs.

By all the saints, when I got to my feet after my praying, I was not a little thankful that my wit had so quickly served me for the nonce, for there, not ten paces behind me, knelt a Mohammedan, who an I had not given heed to the Muedhdhin's call had, I am fully persuaded, straightly suspected my disguise.

At length, and it did seem a lifetime of slow creeping to my impatient feet, I gained the path to which I was tending and with all caution possible and such speed as I could make over the rough way in the dark I stumbled on, fearful at every step lest I had been marked and followed.

After a time I was come to the place of turning off, which place I had had a care to mark in the day by an heap of stones on the roadside. I crept over the stones, stopping now and again to listen if perchance any footstep pressed upon mine own, but all was still. I reached the brambles 'gainst the wall of rock and was about to thrust them aside and squeeze myself through the entrance to the cave, when they stirred of themselves, the hand and arm of a man was come through shortly followed by his body.

I stepped aside quickly; perchance my almost noiseless move caught the man's ear, for as he straightened himself he faced me. I paused not to see if it were friend or foe, for all were alike foes to me in this, but with a swift strong thrust I buried my baselard deep in the fellow's bosom, who without cry or groan dropped to the earth.

Warily I bent over him lest he be but feigning; in the dim light I could faintly discern the lean brown countenance and wolf-like features of mine enemy, Taleb Ebn Amru. Then my soul leaped up with joy, knowing that at last Ronald's death was avenged, and the Emir's evil designs gainst the Soldan come to swift nothingness.

Pausing not so much as to withdraw my baselard from the villain's breast I took my sword within my hand lest another enemy lurk within the way that I must tread. I doubled myself with much effort and squeezed through the narrow opening into the cavern. I bethink me I am no coward when I may face a foe and fight him fairly, but of a truth when I undid myself from crawling through that villainous tight hole, there did play up and down the column of my body a creeping of horror. Each instant I looked to encounter another hand in the darkness or feel a knife-thrust in my body. The blackness was so intense it did seem to rear itself before me forming a barrier through which I might not pass. I paused to listen if there were other movement than mine, but only mine own loud breathing was audible and the rapid sounding of my heart-beats.

I now pressed forward as swiftly as I might, feeling with my hands 'gainst one side of the cavern lest I go astray and wander I know not whither. At length, after what seemed a mighty space of time to my tense nerves, I felt the freshness of the outer world 'gin to make its way 'gainst the foulness of the cavern air, and shortly I was without on the rocky path, stumbling oft, oft falling, nathless making a right fair speed toward the plains below.

Coming to the foot of the hill, I directed my course by the stars. Too well I knew the constellation which hung over the Christian camp; had I not nightly turned toward it as a Mohammedan to his Mecca? I set off then with as much of speed as I deemed wise to begin with, seeing I had a distance of near nine leagues to go.

From time to time I paused to place mine ear 'gainst the earth and listen if perchance I might already hear the faint hoof-beats of the Saracen's horses.

By the course of the stars I judged that one hour must have sped over me, and still no sound of the advancing foe broke on mine ear, though I strained my hearing to catch the smallest noise. On and on I pushed, coming a'ready to be blown and spent, for I was little fitted by my long weeks of sloth to endure this race for life.

And now by the stars I was for believing the second hour passed, when I paused again to lay my ear to the earth. The pulsing of my heart was so thick that for a space of time I was in doubt if other sound came to me, 'til at length there was borne to me, faintly, far away but not to be mistaken, the dull sound of steady galloping feet. Then was I ware that the real race lay before me and what I had done was as a summer pastime to what I must. Springing to my feet I drew the long robe of wool tight up about my middle and with arms close pressed 'gainst my sides, I set out now at a steady run. On and on I sped, the blood beating in my head and my heart sledging 'gainst my ribs 'til it seemed like to crack them. No tarrying now to listen to the sound of mine advancing adversaries, no second of time to be lost an I gain this race for the life of my king.

The darkness was growing deeper as it ever does ere the coming of dawn. Now above the noise of my pounding heart there was come to me the faint far-away thud, thud of the on-coming horses. On, and on, and on, it seemed a lifetime that I had been running thus, when, without word or warning, my great bulk came into swift sharp contact with the earth over which I slipped and sprawled not a little ere I could stay myself, because of the force with which I had fallen. Up to my feet I came again with as little loss of time as might be, only to be ware that my foot had twisted in the fall and each step was now become so grievous that with it there went through my body a pain so great that a cold as of winter passed over me, despite that I did drip of sweat and was as wet as I had fallen into a stream.

Thanks be to the saints, the camp was not

far distant now. I could e'en descry it dimly through the gloom, calm in its sleeping repose.

The sound of the enemies' horse was now distinct on mine ear, though I bethought me that in accordance with their plot they must ere long pause and send forward their assassins. By this I would be enabled to gain somewhat of time. I struggled on, each step a pain a'most beyond enduring, 'til at length I reached the outer edge of the camp.

Having great caution, I passed with stealth through the silent rows of tents toward the great pavilion over which stood the standard of England.

Now must I have a double care, for the Saracen dress, which had been a protection within the camp of Saladin, was now become a menace to me, and did any waking soldier spy me creeping thus amongst the tents, he had quickly sent my soul from me without priest or mass to ease it going.

Now, by the Holy Rood, at length I stood with bounding heart and great thanksgiving before the tent where the king lay. I was even about to make a most unceremonious entrance into the royal presence, when out of the dimness of the dawning day, I felt myself seized in a close grip and the next instant a stinging pain in the arm gave me to know that I had received a knife-thrust there.

I tore myself free of the fellow's grasp, and

ere he could strike again, by a mighty putting forth of my well-nigh spent strength, I grappled with and threw him. My knee firm pressed upon his breast, 'til I could a'most hear the bones of him crack, I at length gained breath wherewith to speak.

"Stay thy rash hand, man, or by St. George, thou 'lt live to sorrow! I am no infidel enemy, as thou art for thinking me, but Godfrey de Bersac come to warn the king of treachery."

On hearing his own tongue so fairly spoken the fellow ceased struggling, and I unfastened my grip of him enough to free one hand. With this I tore from my head the Arab keffieh, and even in the gray-pallid light of dawn 't was plain to see me no Saracen.

Knowing myself safe I was on the instant letting go my hold of the soldier, when the tent curtain was quickly thrust aside, and Richard, roused by the noise of our encounter, stood above me, still clad in the loose linen camisa in which he slept. He had swiftly caught up his sword when the noise wakened him, and now stood with it poised above my head. An I had not looked up as I did, my skull had been quickly riven by such a blow as only Richard knows how to dispense.

"My lord, stay, I beg thee," cried I, springing upright and letting go the soldier with whom I but now contended. "'T is I, Godfrey de Bersac, thy loyal servant, come to warn thee of treachery. Bid the heralds sound the alarm on the instant, and do thou get within thine armor as fleetly as may be. The Saracens be almost upon thee now. I have run the livelong night to reach thee in time," — saying which I sank to the earth exhausted from fatigue and pain of my twisted foot.

Even by this time many of the king's household were aroused, and in less time than I take to word it, I heard the heralds sound forth the warning trumpet, and the cry, "To arms, to arms," rung through the erstwhile silent camp, which straight sprang to vivid life. Torches flamed, men ran hither and yon, the tramp of horses' feet and the neighing of the startled steeds, who scented danger and pawed the earth in anticipation thereof, — all these sounds blended themselves in my almost failing sense.

Some one, I know not who, pressed a flagon into my hand, and when I had turned the good wine with which it brimmed adown my throat, parched to the dryness of a runlet in the summer season, my strength was not a little renewed; and, while Richard was being laced within his armor, I, half sitting, half reclining on the royal couch whence my blood dripped slowly from the wound in my arm, worded to them all the tale of my coming, and the plot to take the king sleeping and slay him, and destroy the half-wakened camp.

When I had made an end of speaking, the king

had such words of commendation for me that, all spent and weary as I was, the blood surged through me with joy as they fell on my ear. "And now," saith he in ending, "if thou art not too greatly spent, get thee from thy infidel garments and into a shirt of mail, and follow me. We will this day give the Saracens to be meat for the fowls of the air."

"Nay, sire, this may not be, for I beg thee to know I must on the instant set out for the Saracen camp again. If thou canst spare a horse to bear me hence, well and good; if not, then of necessity must I fare as best I can afoot. Saphadin, whose prisoner I am, hath my word for it that I will remain safely within his hands until such time as I am ransomed. It therefore becometh me to return thither without delay."

"By St. Hilary, Godfrey, this thou shalt not. Thy life would scarce be worth a fairy-groat an thou go within the infidel's power after thine acts of this night. Beshrew me, thou shalt not go hence an I stay thee by force."

"Say not so, your majesty, for I have ill deserved this. The life of Godfrey de Bersac is of little worth; an he were willing to outlive his honor, 't would be much less, withal. Besides the which, I have good hope to reach the camp ere Saphadin return, and perchance this night's work may not come to his ears 'til I myself word it to him, which being so, he will have somewhat to thank me for himself, seeing that the treachery of the Emir was toward Saladin as well as toward thee."

"Thou hast the right of me in this, noble youth, and I cry you pardon for my ill speaking. It shall be as thou hast said. Take the best horse that thou canst find and make all speed possible. The sooner you come within the Saracen camp the less hast thou to fear. Howbeit, bear this in mind, if the infidel dogs so much as harm a hair of thy head, Richard shall take such vengeance on them that the earth will ring of it. Now the saints have good care toward thee," — saying which the king, being now full-armed, passed in haste from the pavilion, while I made my way without to where the horses were, for choosing a steed to bear me back to the Saracen camp.

Already the soldiers were armed and mounting, and I needs must take such beast as I could, for but few remained from which to make choice. I was about to fling myself on the back of a strong black destrier, who looked to have little of speed in his heavy hocks, but of a truth seemed the best that I could do for myself, when I felt a cold, velvet-soft muzzle thrust within my hand, and turning I beheld the a'most human eyes of Mohammed gazing within mine own.

Perchance 't was because of the happenings of this night, which had in some sort put me without my wonted calm, that caused the water to spring to mine eyes ere I was ware of it. For, gazing on the beast, I seemed to see Ronald, as he stood beside him on the day of my riding from camp with the king. I beheld again that look of loving fear which followed after me, and a mighty pain gripped my heart, and on a sudden turned me weakling. I loosed my hold of the horse I was but now mounting, and, flinging my leg over the back of Mohammed, turned his head from camp and put him to his speed. He was over-light to bear my weight, I knew, but I had little time now to think of this, and it did a'most seem to me, as I felt the horse beneath my knees, bounding forward with such willing strides, that Ronald was himself come again to help me with the same loving service as of old.

Ere I was any distance from camp I heard the wild shout of the Turks, which they ever utter as they go into battle. The answering cry, " St. George, St. George," came clear from many hundred English throats, and the earth trembled and dindled under the shock of battle.

The blood flew burning to my finger ends for longing to be in the fray. Mohammed pressed on, nothing heeding, in a swift, steady gallop, seeming to bear me gladly, while I sat turned about in my saddle, gazing toward the field of battle, where hung a cloud of dust turned now to glorious brightness by the slow-rising sun.

On and on we galloped, 'til the din of battle came but faintly to us, being in the end swallowed up in heavy silence. Then was I come aware that, what from want of sleep and weariness of my night race, the pain of my leg and loss of blood from my arm, I was well-nigh dropping from Mohammed's back, and must continually arouse me lest I fall on sleep and roll helpless to the earth. I kept the beast's head well toward the purple line of hills which we were ever nearing, and pressed on fleetly, though every moment found mine eyes more holden with sleep.

After a time, in which I bethink me I must have drowsed upright upon the horse's back — for there doth seem to be a blank in my thoughts when I would recall anything — I was come suddenly to my sense by taking a mighty tumble over Mohammed's neck and falling none so softly 'gainst the rocky earth.

I gathered me up stifly, every bone o' me lamenting grievously at this sudden shaking. Turning, I beheld Mohammed still prone upon the earth, having a look well-nigh human in his suffering eyes. Nor could the poor brute rise; and I was not long in seeing that he had unwitting stuck his foot within the hole of some ground animal, and in his fall had snapped the slender bone of his leg as it had been a dry twig.

The faithful beast turned his soft grieving eyes on me as he did sorrow more for that he had failed me than for his own poor plight.

Beshrew me, man though I was, I could have wept at sight of him and for knowing what I perforce must do. I could not leave the beast to live and suffer, perchance to be devoured alive by the carrion birds of the air. Slay him I must, though, by all the saints, it did seem like the murder of a Christian.

I drew the long sleek head 'gainst my knee; stroking it softly, I talked to him as he had been human.

"Mohammed, I am for sending thee on a long and happy journey. Thou shalt go this day to thy little master, who hath great need of thee, I trow, in the other land where she has gone before. Say to her, to my gentle little comrade, that I do bear her ever in mind, and that no service of hers is forgot," — saying which I swift plunged my sword into the beast's heart and stopped its pulsing on the instant.

I closed his fast glazing eyes with gentle hand and thanked the saints that they gazed upon me only lovingly — for had they worn within their depths a look of reproach, I think I had then and there turned my sword on myself, so sorry was my mood, so jaded was I in body and spirit.

I would not take up my journey 'til I had fetched enough of stones wherewith to cover the body of the horse, for I could not of my pity leave it to the ravening wolves and the sharp beaks of the birds.

Having finished this task, I took up my painful way toward the hill, which, the Virgin be praised, was not now far distant.

I crept on, each step an agony, 'til I was at length come to the rocky path 'twixt the two hills, which I clambered slowly, with much labor and weariness.

At last I had passed the cave, pushed my way through hole and past bramble, and stood once more within the limit of the Saracen camp. I looked about me for the body of Taleb Ebn Amru. It was nowhere visible, but a deep brown stain on rock and earth told me that 'twas no dream of mine that I had struck him down here, and here avenged Ronald's death. Scarce more than twelve hours agone was it since this deed, yet it did seem as a lifetime had rolled over me since last I stood upon this spot.

Pausing not to meditate of what had befallen the body of my foe or where he was, I took my way toward the camp, which no sooner was I come anear than I was most rudely seized by a band of soldiers, and with no gentle handling, haled to the great pavilion, into the presence of Saladin and Saphadin.

My garments torn and soiled, the blood from my wounded arm clotted in brown streaks upon me, brier scratched on hands and face, dust-grimed, the stain on my face streaked with little runlets of sweat, I made but a sorry figure to bear myself with the proud-crested air that the occasion warranted. Nathless, I tried to stand upright and hold myself aloft as ever, though of a truth I perforce bore heavily on the shoulders of my captors, else had I fallen.

The pavilion was thronged, and mine eye took account of many of Taleb Ebn Amru's kinsmen and tribesmen, who wore no gentle look, and they cast eyes on me, and 'mongst whom there passed a wolfish growl which gave me to know they thirsted mightily for such of my blood as remained to me. In the midst of the pavilion, stretched on the earth, lay the body of the dead Emir, with my baselard still sticking in his breast and a look of horrid fright frozen on his dead face.

Saphadin's look met mine, and within it there was so much of contempt it cut me as a lash, and left little need of the words which he straightly uttered on seeing me.

"Is it thus, Sir Knight, that a Christian keeps his word? An infidel had felt himself disgraced in this."

Like strong liquor in my veins was the reproach of the Saracen. I pushed aside the two soldiers on whom I leaned and stood proudly forward.

"I beg thee to know, noble Saphadin, and thou, most mighty Soldan, that naught but mine own will compelled me hence to place my life in jeopardy of thee. Because of my acts, thou canst take it if, having heard that which I would say to thee, thou art desirous of so doing," quoth I, bearing myself right proudly despite my state.

Saladin pointed to the body of the dead Emir. Saith he, "Is not this thy baselard, dog of a Christian, and this being so canst thou face us thus?"

"Ay, my lord, it is my baselard, and never did it better service for thee or me than when it struck home to its present abiding-place."

"Dost thou name it good service to me to slay my powerful allies?" saith he sternly.

"Nay, but to slay thy powerful enemies I do, and such was Taleb Ebn Amru, a forsworn dishonored dog," quoth I hotly.

"Have a care what thou sayest an thou canst not make good thy speech, Christian," saith he as hotly, whilst the kinsmen of the dead Emir made as if to tear me in shreds, giving forth again that wolfish blood-thirsting growl.

"But give me leave to word my tale to thee, my lord, and listen to me with patience an thou'lt hear me make good all that I have maintained."

Whereupon he bade me speak, and I began at the hour yestermorn when by a miracle of God's working I was led to pause beside the crevice in the rock, whence had come to mine ear the evil schemes of Taleb Ebn Amru and his ally the Marquis of Montserrat; and step by step I did recount to him all my doings, from the hour in which I buried my baselard deep in the villain's breast to the instant when I was haled before him wounded and half dead.

"If thou hadst been within the camp, noble Soldan, this had not been, for I had straight borne this news to thine ear, and trusted thee to save the king of England from this most foul treachery; but thou wert abroad, and no instant of time to be lost an I save the life of my king. What could I save that which I did?" saith I, when at length I did reach the conclusion of the matter.

"What proof hast thou of the truth of thy tale?" the Soldan then demanded of me.

"Naught save my word, but I deem it most like if thou wilt have the body of the Emir searched that thou wilt find upon him the parchments which the messenger brought but yestermorn from Conrad of Montserrat."

At a sign from the Soldan, two slaves bent to the task, and 'twas shortly discovered, as I had hoped. My baselard had even stuck through the very spot of their resting, pinioning the parchments to the traitor's breast.

When the Soldan had made an end of examining the bloodstained writings, he turned toward me.

"Thou hast proved all thy speech, noble Christian, and hast done Saladin far greater service than that of saving him from treachery.

For I had rather the loss of half my kingdom than that mine honor should have borne the stain of such an attempt on the life of Malec Ric. As for this carrion," and he stirred the dead Emir with his foot, "bear it hence from my sight, and you his kinsmen, forget it not that I will shortly reckon with you as ye deserve."

After which, I shame not to say it, I fell to the floor, nor knew aught for many days, during which time I was most tenderly cared for in the household of Saphadin.

When I was come to mine own wit again — but still weak and helpless withal — it gave me no little joy to find my friend oft beside my couch, and to be ware that he deemed me no longer in fault for my acts, but rather did hold that I had paid in full all kindness received of his hands.

And this be the proper end of my tale, being, as it was, the end of my adventures. No great while was it after this that the truce 'twixt the Christians and Saracens was made; a truce to last three years, three months, three weeks, three days, and three hours.

Thus, when my ransom was come, all fighting was at an end.

When next I saw my lord the king, he was scarce able to stand, being but new arisen from a bed of sickness, which came near to carrying him swiftly from the world.

I dropped upon my knee before him, joy at once more beholding him well-nigh choking speech.

"Your gracious majesty, I desire to return thanks to thee for thy generous ransom."

"By my faith, Godfrey, I bethink me the balance doth still tip heavily in thy favor. I know not if Richard returns to a kingdom or a prison," — his words faltered an instant. "'Tis said that during our absence our brother John hath seized upon our sceptre. If I come to mine own again — nay, Richard speaks as a weakling — *when* I am come to mine own, thou 'lt see that thy king hath a long memory toward those who serve him." Then most sadly: "the Crusade hath come to an end, and mine eyes have yet to behold Jerusalem conquered. This truce of three years is all. The mountain hath travailed, the silly mouse hath come forth."

"Nay, never speak in such heavy tone, my lord, I pray thee. Richard is not himself in this. Thou hast done all that mortal could with thy many hindrances."

He waved my words aside, for his mood did not fit them. Saith he, "From henceforward thou shalt bear on thy coat armor the lions of England. Thou hast fairly merited them. There be some who bear a king's heart, Godfrey de Bersac, who wear not a king's crown, and such thy deeds have proclaimed thee. Take then for thy motto thine own generous words, 'Je suis le Roi.'"

III

ANSELM'S TALE

I, Anselm de Bersac, brother to Sir Godfrey and chaplain at Weregrave, have, at my lady's command, writ down the foregoing tales, she being minded that the deeds of their sire shall still be had in remembrance of the children who come after.

It now becometh my task to take up this tale which Marian hath let fall, and to finish the chronicle. Albeit, 'tis but a holiday task to pen the words of another, yet withal I am sore let and hindered when I would word mine own part thereof. I am for beginning at the hour of my coming to Weregrave, but to this my lady saith a downright "nay," it being her whimsey that I speak something of mine own life first, and I, not minded to withstand her in aught, must needs yield me. Howbeit, there is naught of concern to other in those dull sad days of mine upgrowing. Shall I tell thee of that day when, scarce four summers old, I unwitting crept too near my father's horse ere he rode from the court to the hunt, or of how the jennet did fetch me a blow with its iron-shod heel and brake the bone o' my leg, which when the barber surgeon had set, it did mend crookedly, leaving me misshapen and halting for life? Or shall I break silence of those after days when there did war within my young soul a spirit of fierce unrest and hate to all save Godfrey, for that being a weakling none looked on me as man or fit for aught save priestly garb? Or yet later, when I came to be cothy,[1] and to hate even mine own self for that I did ever dream and long to do valorous deeds, but did occasion for the same arise my weakling body would flinch aside, making me coward in act?

Godfrey it was, the bravest of my kin, who had patience of mine infirmity and flung no gibe at me for that I was coward, and thus led me at length to such poor manliness as I now can boast. At best 'tis but a sorry likeness of a real thing, and oft my bitter spirit is constrained to say with the psalmist, "I am no man, a worm, a very scorn of men." Having been other than this how had I lived and borne to see my lady suffer at the hands of Sir Hugh that which she did?

Nay, I must of my judgment withstand my lady and pass from all this to the hour of my coming to Weregrave, else will I burst forth into raving hate of myself once more.

[1] Morose.

As thou art ware, Hugh de Hardecute was my kinsman, and thus when my priesting was accomplished I right gladly embraced his offer to be chaplain unto my lady, which offer was come shortly after the death of Lady Joscelyn's father and Sir Hugh's removal from his own great castle of Hardecute to Weregrave Manor, which though not so spacious seemed nathless to better please his wayward fancy.

'T was a fair day and warm of the season when first I rode within the Manor court. Something of confusion there was about, and not a few stoneworkers and woodworkers still lingered, having scarce completed the task of rebuilding the half-ruined place. When I was come into the great hall where my kinsman commanded me wait upon him, beshrew me, I hated him on that instant. Though the hour of tierce was some time passed, he was not yet come from his drinking. He sat, slipped down within his seat, grasping an empty flagon whose contents he had but now gulped down, as the ruddy stream on his beard did testify. He was large of stature and something handsome, despite that excess of liquor had a'ready distended his bulk, giving him a heavy paunch, and even growing deep folds of flesh about his purple face. I wot not where Hugh came of this drunken thirst, save from his Saxon ancestry. For be it known to you that Sir Hugh's father had got him a Saxon heiress to wife, and by this had well propped the falling fortunes of his house. But for myself I like not the Saxon blood, which doth ever seem to tend to such excess as we of Norman race contemn.

When Sir Hugh had looked me coolly over with his half-closed, drink-glazed eyes, my slight stature, my halting gait my a'most womanish countenance, all, he took note on with an evil sneering curl of lip, which having done he burst into a hoarse roar of mirth that well-nigh shook the Manor walls.

"So," saith he, when he had made an end of his drunken laughter, — "so thou art our new chaplain and cousin beside? By the Holy Rood! thou art well fitted for hearing confessions and mumbling prayers. Of a truth, being so much woman thyself thou art not like to do great damage 'mongst the wenches. Belike thou 'lt serve as well and be as little harmful in this as the old dotard who hath held the place since before the hour of my coming to this earth. Thou shouldst have seen the old abbey-lubber[1] drivel and plead that I do not turn him forth from his soft quarters. St. George! but 't was rare sport, and thou wouldst have doubled thyself with mirth to see the twisting and trembling of his spindle legs an he essayed to bend them and kneel in supplication at my feet. Pah! I like not the thought o' him, and I be happily rid of the sight, which did ever

[1] Lazy, idle fellow.

bring me to think of grave-damps and worms, which things I like not to dwell upon. An thou serve me long, Sir Chaplain, keep young and lusty, or I am like to kick thee forth with small ceremony. Get thee gone now; Giles will show thee to thy chamber, and anon my lady will set thee to thy tasks, and the saints be witness, I care not what they be." And with that he 'gan to pound the board and shout to his cup-man that he fill his flagon fleetly, naming the fellow between whiles a string of foul names of which Saxon swineherd was the gentlest and most full of courtesy.

Such my coming to Weregrave, and such my welcome from my cousin. I turned aside from the drunken wastrel to follow Giles, all the poor manliness in me rising up to hate and contempt. Weakling though I be, I held him the sorrier of us twain.

I dare be sworn I had straightly ridden from Weregrave that day, nor ever shadowed its walls again an it had not been for a later happening which fell out thus.

Giles having gone from my chamber, leaving me alone, there grew within me the resolve to be gone in the hour, though of a truth I knew not whither. A hot rage so burned within me that I was for seeking the open air, where my communing with myself seems ever clearer. Having passed without, I came upon the garden which yet no pruning-hand had touched, it being scarce more than a tangle of briers. Pacing the walk, I heeded not where my unknowing feet were bearing me, 'til on a sudden I beheld the narrow path had widened to a small court round which the branches reared an enclosing wall. Within this spot a circular bench of stone was set, and from its middle the gray face of a sun-dial showed itself. Kneeling on the rim of the bench, with face low buried in the bended arm a-resting on the dial, was a maiden. So deep in grief was she that her ear had not caught my coming step. Her couvre-chief was cast aside, and her long glittering braids fell 'gainst the stone, down, down, 'til they brushed the red and russet leaves on the sward below. Over against the damsel a dark yew-tree, once cut to the semblance of a griffin, bent threateningly, seeming about to spring upon her and rend her with its gaping mouth.

I paused, waiting 'til she was minded to raise her head, while she, thinking her that none was anear, moaned and moaned like a dumb creature which hath its death hurt.

If it had so happed that I had crept thence unheeded, as I was minded to do, all after life had been another thing for me; howbeit her helpless grief so wrought upon my heart I needs must offer her some poor comfort.

"Child," quoth I, a-laying my hand upon her bended head, "the peace of God be with thee. Thou hast brought thy sorrows to the surest healer. Time hath a cure for all wounds, be they as deep as they may."

With a frighted cry she started from beneath my hand and stood upright. I saw two eyes like brimming seas of sorrow, and a face which then, as now, I cannot set before you save in the words of the psalmist: "Thou art fairer than the daughters of men, full of grace are thy lips." And again with Solomon, who doth describe his beloved thus: "Thy teeth are like a flock of sheep that are even shorn, which come up from the washing: whereof every one bear twins and none is barren among them. Thy lips are like a thread of scarlet, and thy speech is comely: thy temples are like a piece of pomegranate within thy locks."

A long minute were her eyes holden to mine, while the color fled her face, leaving it of an awful whiteness. "Man or spirit, where got you Godfrey's eyes?" saith she at length in choked voice.

"Nay, lady, be not so frighted," quoth I in amaze at her; "I am no spirit, but flesh and blood as thou. I am the chaplain but new come at Weregrave."

"Thy name, thy name?" quoth she, a mighty tremble seizing upon her.

"Anselm de Bersac, my lady."

"De Bersac, de Bersac!" cried she. "Thou hast a brother?"

"Ay, if he be not dead he wears the white cross in Palestine."

Then uttered she a cry as I had driven a knife deep within her heart straight followed by a look I know not how to tell thee on. Her hands flew out toward me like two swift fluttering doves. "Thou wilt be my friend, wilt help me, cousin?" saith she, surpassing sweetness in her tone; but ere I could grasp her hands or answer, swearing to her the fealty which on the instant sprung like a fountain in my heart, she had withdrawn them and clasped them over her face, murmuring the while in broken accents, "Nay, nay, 't is wicked, I cannot, I dare not." Saying which she dropped upon the stone bench, drooping as a broken flower. "Good sir, I cry you pardon for my unmannerliness and beg you begone. I am out of myself, and being such am not responsible. By and by I will come to mine own mind once again, 'til then I pray you begone and leave me."

Still in amaze, knowing not in what I had offended, I turned from her, but as I took my halting way from the spot, my heart lay heavy and sore within me, as it had ne'er before done for the sorrow of other. I knew beyond the peradventure of a doubt that despite my cousin Hugh or my hatred of him, I was henceforward as fast holden at Weregrave as I were some base Saxon slave and no longer free man.

So came about the beginning of my life at Weregrave. Of the days and months which followed I would I could hold silence, for my heart doth burn at memory of them, even though the time be now far distant: howbeit, my tale would fail of completeness told I not of them.

How can I give thee to know what life was to my lady, an I cannot set before thee the man she called lord; and words do choke me when I essay the task. One merit only had he, if merit thou couldst name it, — he was not niggard with his gold; but bethink you, even heaven-born charity could scarce be counted virtue, an it were found in such base company.

Marian, who is my lady's foster-sister and tire-woman, hath told me much of the great change which Sir Hugh's coming hath wrought in the Manor. Tapestry hangs now 'gainst the bare chamber walls, stained glass fills the lattice where a thurl cloth had used to stop the weather, and skins of animals cunningly dressed cover the once bare floor. Weregrave keeps fast no more, nor knows aught of hungry paunches.

All this were greatly for the better, look ye; an it had not been for Sir Hugh himself, life had been a summer holiday. But and if the master of the Manor scarce draw a sober breath, and if beside he be cothy in his cups and ever ready to lay on blows with a right good will — even my lady, I sometimes fear; but of that I'll e'en be silent.

What recks it, say I, an there be plenty in the larder, if there be not room for peace?

Naught on the place had respect to the master thereof, not even the hound that crouched to his feet. Thou shouldst have heard him, after his pottle-deep potations, boast of the knightly deeds he had done an he went to the Crusades. Ne'er had a Saracen lived beyond the hour of encounter, for an he had not died of blows he had fallen of fright at sight of his doughty enemy. His own retainers were at no pains to hide their smiles or cover their quips afore their pot-valiant lord an he reached this stage of vaunting, and many time hath my lady's cheek burned hot an she caught some passing look.

All things base seemed best to please Sir Hugh; ribald songs he did delight to have his minstrels sing after the hour of dinner; an did my lady desire to go from the hall and be out of ear of it, he straight commanded her be seated, for that 'twas pain to her.

Seldom did she array her will 'gainst his, but an she did, she ever conquered. I say 't was ever thus save when he was totty and far gone in drink; then not even the look in her shining eyes would daunt him. Once do I remember, 'twas when Sir Hugh had commanded two lusty knaves lay fifty stripes on the bare back of poor Clement, for that he had unwitting driven a nail to the quick in shoeing Sir Hugh's favorite jennet. Then it was that my lady stood 'gainst him; though it was not that which she uttered so much as the look which she cast on him that saved a whole skin to poor Clement that day.

"Death of my life, my lady, and is it that I am to let that nidering Saxon hind ruin my best jennet and go unscathed to please thy whimsey? By all the saints i' the calendar, and the devils who bear no place amongst such pious sort, thou dotest."

"I dote not, my lord. Thou knowest well that Clement's fault lieth with the infirmity of age. He hath served my father long and well, and is now beyond the point of work. Thou shouldst get thee a younger farrier, and turn the old horse to field with plenty to fill him and naught to do," saith she, with that look bent on him that I did tell thee on.

"By Sathanus, thou wouldst have me feed a pack of lazy varlets who ne'er turn hand to work, because, forsooth, they served thy old dotard of a father," quoth he; "but that I will not," — and he turned from her, seeking to be free of her gaze.

Nathless, Clement was not flogged, and a younger farrier took his place.

Howbeit, though in defence of other my lady did sometimes oppose her lord, in all else she submitted to him, as she had no will or wish of her own. At all times she bore herself with a calm which was not akin to peace. She ordered her household as befitted her station, and saw that the maidens learned spinning, weaving, and stitchery. With her own hands she daily fed her lord's hawks, which he kept on a perch in his chamber, and sometimes she did even bear one on her gloved fist;[1] but 'twas seldom, she seeming to mislike the birds and care naught for the sport.

On a time when Sir Hugh questioned her of this and of why she joyed not in falconry as other noble dames, she made answer with a smile his wine-fuddled wits could scarce interpret, "Belike 't is that I have too keen a knowledge of what the bird doth suffer in the falcon's clutch."

Ay, that had she, poor young thing.

To none spake she of Sir Hugh, nor uttered complaint of aught, and on a day when Marian of her fulness burst forth with lamentation because of her lady's sorry lot, she did chide her soundly and bid her remember that life was but a cherry fair and the longest day soon lived out.

Toward me, my lady bore herself with gentle considerateness, which nathless varied from a loving friendliness to distant kindliness in such fashion as to sorely puzzle my poor wit. Never

---

[1] It was the custom of those who engaged in falconry to carry their hawks as constantly as possible. Old writers on the sport advise this strongly, even insisting that they be taken on the walk abroad and to church, that thus they may become accustomed to crowds. As no one but the gentry was privileged to hawk, a hawk on the fist became a sign of gentility.

tired she of hearkening to my silly talk of boyhood. Oft, indeed, would she gently cozen me to such foolish babbling, but now I do recall that to which I ne'er gave heed at the time, that her interest was ever keen when I spake of Godfrey, or of his prankish ways; of how, when he was scarce twice the size of the bird itself, he did steal my father's hawk and go a-hawking, and on being found many hours after astray and lost in the dark, half dead with fright and weariness, he still clutched the heavy bird to his fist like a right valiant sportsman; of his gentleness to mine infirmity; of all that appertained to him; but, did my discourse wander to Balderic or Drogo, flagged my lady's interest in my speech right quickly.

All this I do remember now, as also I do mind that it was ever after such conversing that my lady constrained herself toward me, as if, poor child, she held herself guilty in something for that she had given ear to harmless tales of her lover's childish goodness.

Much hath Marian, who is passing garrulous, told me of my lady's marriage and what led thereto, but withal, I now am ware that despite her idle chatter, which did seem to say all, she yet withheld much from my knowledge.

So three years ran by, bringing us at length to the hour of Godfrey's coming from the Holy Wars; which falling on us unawares, was like to have been the cause of great disaster, partly because of Marian's silly prating and partly because of the hot youth of my brother.

Sir Hugh had commanded, as oft he did, that I ride with him to the hunt on this day of which I speak, and we were galloping adown the highroad at a nimble pace toward Weregrave forest, followed at some distance by the huntsmen and the dogs, close leashed. Let me have out with it now; though thou scorn me for it, 't is a sport I like not. Many is the night that sleep hath forsaken my pillow for that the sorrowing look in the fast-glazing eyes of a dying deer hath so haunted my vision. I desire not to kill any of God's innocent creatures, though there be some, counted amongst His best creation, over whose passing I had not had this great squeamishness. So I was for wishing myself back with penner and inkhorn over my parchments, when I beheld in the distance two horsemen galloping fleetly toward us.

Nearer they drew and nearer, 'til, beholding them closely, I spurred forward with a shout of joy, for I saw the face of the knight, and it was Godfrey, — Godfrey grown older and wearing a skin changed to burnished copper from the Eastern suns, — Godfrey with a soft look in his eyes, as if joy waited him at the next turn o' the road.

Ere I had made an end of my greeting, Sir Hugh fell on him boisterously. "By my faith, cousin, thou art monstrously welcome. 'T were a right kinsmanly act so soon to turn thy face toward us."

"Gramercy to thee, Hugh, for thy loving welcome, but I ride not to thy castle this day. My business lies at Weregrave, in the keeping of whose lord I have intrusted a something which I go now to claim," quoth Godfrey, with a laugh which seemed to brim with content.

"Then canst thou do thy business and visit thy kinsman at one time, for Weregrave doth hold me now, or I it," quoth Hugh in answer, at which a look flashed in Godfrey's face as all were not well.

"Sir Ralph," questioned he, and I bethought me his voice was scarce as steady or so full of content as it had been, "where dwells he now?"

"By all the saints, of that I cannot inform thee. 'T is there or there," and Hugh did point first up, then down, and break into the senseless laugh ever ready to his lips. "Best ask of thy brother his direction, since he doth have a care of the road by which he passed."

"Dead," quoth Godfrey as one mazed, "and thou perhaps hast wed the lady Joscelyn his daughter?" he questioned, and a new note was now come to his voice.

"Ay, or bought her, as thou mayest say. 'T is much the same with wenches in these times. None are minded to withstand the shine of gold. But why stand we here prating in the highroad? The hunt shall go and we will to Weregrave, cousin, where thy company will mightily enliven our dulness. Come." Which saying, he turned about and put spurs to his jennet.

I could not see Godfrey's face when he turned to follow, but an I did, it was covered with a hard calm, and an evil sneering curled the corner of his lips. I saw beside that the gauntletted hand which hung at his side was clinched as he longed to dash it in the face of some one. By the feeling in my own breast 't was no hard matter to say whom he did desire to serve thus.

When we clattered at length within the court at Weregrave and were dismounted, my lady came forth to learn why we were so soon returned, and thereupon, standing in the great doorway of the Manor, at the top of the broad stair which leads up from the court, she beheld Godfrey. Gazing down on him with wide, frighted eyes, she went as white as the gown of cendal which she wore and dropped the great bunch of gillyflowers that she had but now culled in the garden. I know not what would ha' come of this meeting — for Sir Hugh, though a dolt, was not wholly blind — save that Godfrey bore himself with such quiet as helped my lady to her wonted calm.

Up the stair he passed quickly, his head thrown back, gazing spellbound upon her — and of a truth she had more the look of spirit than of flesh — 'til his stalwart shoulders cut her slight form from our view. Bending, he saluted her on one cheek and on the other, which, being her kinsman, it was his right to. Sir Hugh, who liked not long to be silent, broke forth, saying:

"Thy kinsman, my lady, hath it that he did intrust a something to thy father's keeping when he joined the Crusades, and not knowing him dead, he comes but now to claim his own. Knowest thou aught of this matter?"

"Sir, I cry you grace," saith my lady in tone most low, turning now to Godfrey; "thy property hath been destroyed in the storm and stress which hath gone over our house. I trust in time another shall make good to thee thy little loss."

"Ay, Godfrey, she says rightly; but name the value of thy goods and thou shalt have it and more," quoth Hugh, clapping his shoulder with a rough good-fellowship.

Then did Godfrey, because of his pain and a certain wantonness which man doth ever hold within himself, howsoever much he love, make a most despiteful answer.

"Nay, by the Holy Cross, cousin, thou hast the wrong of it. The thing I spoke on hath no value, nor ever had i' truth, and 't would not be worth the bearing hence an you had it for me. 'T was but gentle courtesy which brought me to demand it."

But an if Godfrey thought thus to make my lady flinch or cry aloud, he had scant knowledge of her. She raised her now calm eyes to his, while she made a deep obeisance, which yet held nothing of humility in it, saying, "I thank thee for thine absolving, my lord."

Sir Hugh stood by, gazing on these two with gowking look, his poor wit no little puzzled. "I know not what thou wouldst, with thy whiffling way of 'come to fetch' and 'will not take,'" saith he with a round and ribald oath. "Take that thine is, man, and have no more words of it;" and so saying, he passed into the Manor hall, where he straightly 'gan to call in no patient voice for wine.

'T was not until after candle-lighting and Godfrey had sought me in mine own apartment that I had occasion of speaking apart with him.

Through the supper hour his speech was barbed and cruel; many a quip he let fly at damsels who forgot love and faith for gold. Sir Hugh drank deep, and was shortly come to the state wherein his wine spake in him, in much loud vaunting, which an it did, my lady's cheek burned to such a mighty red I greatly feared the blood would burst forth, and was not sorry when the wastrel, overcome with his potation, tumbled forward on the table in drunken sleep, blowing such mighty, puffing breaths through his great nostrils that the flagons and pots were made to dance on the board.

Despite that Godfrey's words were sharp, I nathless caught his glance ever fixed on my lady's face when he thought him unobserved. There was within this look much of love and tenderness, which did seem to war with hate and fury.

When he was come within my chamber and the portal closed behind him, he turned upon me with surpassing bitterness in his tone.

"Anselm, what doest thou here? This hell-plagued spot is no fit place for thy gentle soul to dwell. Thou must go hence with me on the morrow."

"Nay, brother, that I may not," I made answer.

"How now, what binds thee to that drunken wastrel?"

"Naught; but to my lady everything."

"So she hath caught thy loyalty also that she may make sport of it, hath she?" quoth he with an evil sneer.

With that, rancor mounted to my brain. I struck my doubled hand upon the oaken desk before me with such force that the skin brake and the blood burst from it, dripping unheeded on my outspread parchments.

"Nay, never look at me thus, Godfrey, or use such foul insult toward my lady, else will I be moved to forget that the same mother gave suck to us. What hath Joscelyn done to thee that thou shouldst so despitefully use her?"

"She but pledged me her love, vowing to await my coming from Palestine, and ere I was fairly set forward on my journey she did wed with another, who had gold and lacked honor; one she herself did openly flout before me. What say you of this, — was it honestly done?" and I was ware from his tone how greatly he suffered in speaking thus.

Nathless, when these words fell on my ear, though I was not far from the knowledge that it had been thus betwixt these two, something, I know not what, or hate or envy, seemed to take my heart into a mighty grip. I watched the heavy red drops fall from my wounded hand, gather to a little pool and turn to a slow-moving tiny dark stream, and while my thought seemed only to heed this small matter, somewhere beneath another self was going over my poor life and setting it beside Godfrey's, — Godfrey who had strong limbs and love-winning ways, — Godfrey who had earned a king's favor and bore not a few of honorable scars; and this beside was added unto him — my lady's love. For I doubted not that 't was his even yet. My memory went back to the hour of first seeing her beside the dial; her pale face and broken words at sight of me: "Man or spirit, where got you Godfrey's eyes?" 'T was for this that she had been most loving, gentle toward me, forsooth, because I wore Godfrey's eyes; 't was for this that she wearied not of my silly tales of boyhood, because they told her of Godfrey's boyhood beside. Almost I hated him, I know not how or why, save that man's nature is ever base and envious, and likes not to see another obtain a larger measure of life than he can compass for himself. Godfrey's voice broke upon my envious musing.

"Thou art long silent, — hast thou then naught of excuse for her?" and his voice did bewray his hope and disappointment.

"Only this, my brother," quoth I: "had such an one pledged faith with me I had not lightly contemned her."

"God's mercy, man, if thou knowest aught that will lighten her blame, if ever so little, tell it me; I do beseech thee tell it me," saith he, grasping my blooded hand, nor heeding the crimson stain it left upon his own, while I could see a shimmering lamp of hope light itself in the blue depths of his eyes.

To my lips there sped a mighty rush of words in defence of my lady; an I had not checked them quickly, I had straightly unfolded to him all that I knew and much that I guessed. But wisdom bade me be silent, for an this hot-blooded soldier knew all that I was ware of, the consequence was like to be sorry enough for all, and most so for my lady, who could a-better bear his spite than his tenderness. So I only shook my head in reluctant denial and watched the light die slowly from my brother's eyes and the old look of hardness come in them again.

On the next day he made excuse of departing, the which Hugh turned aside nor would hear of. Goddot,[1] 'twas hard to say if Godfrey had been able to word to himself that which he most desired — to abide or depart. Nathless, he remained, tormenting himself sorely and treating my lady ever despitefully; though ofttimes he did bewray his heart in the looks which he bent upon her.

'Twas a week o' the day of his coming to Weregrave when Marian sought my chamber weeping and bewailing her for that which she had done and was now fain to have undone.

Naught could I drag from her of her fault 'til patience was well-nigh worn through; she being scant of breath for that she used it all a-calling down upon her pate such monstrous punishments. I dare be sworn an she had seen the first one coming, she had on the instant showed herself a right nimble footman.

"Body o' me, body o' me, why came I ever into the world?" quoth she, still lamenting, rocking to this side and that with face buried deep in her kirtle.

Saith I, my patience now clean gone, "That

---

[1] An oath or exclamation common in early writers, and evidently an abbreviation of God wot, or God knows.

I wot not, Marian, an it were not to drive lunatic any who would gain sane speech of thee."

At length, when I was well-nigh at the end of my wit because of her, she spake, weeping bitterly the while and pausing oft to bewail herself for a shatterpated fool. "God pardon, that I should take it upon me to do that which my lady saw fit to leave undone; but think you I could a-bear to let Sir Godfrey speak lightly of my pretty one when she so ill deserved it? So this morn I made occasion to speak apart with him, and unfolded the whole tale of her marrying, nor spared a full picture of Sir Hugh and what she had suffered of him; and when I had made an end of speaking, beshrew me, I was regretful that I had not followed my lady's example and kept silence, for the man did rave as he had lost his wit.

"He was by turns for killing Sir Hugh or carrying my lady off bodily and defying the coward to his worst. Long it was ere I coaxed him to his wit again and forced him see that he could do naught, for that my lady would be first to punish his rash acts."

"Thou hast well named thyself a shatterpated fool in this, Marian," quoth I with sternness, when she had made an end of speaking and sat on the floor in a huddled heap, fetching long breaths and murmuring to the Virgin for forgiveness of her fault. "If my lady had knowledge of thy folly, I know not what she would have in store for thee."

At hearing this Marian's sobs burst forth afresh and loudly.

"Good Sir Chaplain, good Sir Anselm, as thou dost hope mercy for thyself, word not my fault to her. She will have no hard word for Marian, this I know right well, but I cannot a-bear to have her looks turned from me in displeasure:" and, lest I be drowned in the salt water from Marian's eyes, I needs must promise to hold my speech in regard to the matter.

The wench had scarce departed, having first had, I promise you, a sound rating for her meddlesome tongue, when Godfrey himself came, with a look on him such as I ne'er hope to see upon any man's face again. For a good hour by the dial he raged and blasphemed 'til 'twas disgrace to the cross he wore. At first I did essay to stem the torrent of his wrath, but words were as straws i' the wind. Perforce I waited 'til his temper had wrought something of exhaustion in him, then with as much of wisdom as I knew I led him to see that the acts which he did threat would but forever cast him from my lady's presence.

Never more may I see such sight, for in the end he brake down, and hard sobs rent his great frame as he had been a little child, and this not because of himself, but for his impotence to make my lady's lot one whit the easier.

"Thou knowest not what things I suffer, Anselm. How canst thou? What comfort hath thy religion for such pain as this?" he made bitter challenge of me after a time. To which I could but shake my head and answer "None." For it hath ever seemed passing strange to me that whereas the Lord Christ healed sickness and blindness, brought the dead to life, suffered poverty, loneliness, and grievous pain in his own body, he yet left no word of comfort for the heaviest sorrow which mankind doth suffer.

Worse was yet to follow on Marian's foolish babbling. As I did foresee, Godfrey's manner toward my lady changed. Whereas he had been cold and despiteful, now was he all gentleness.

All this so worked upon her calm that she was well-nigh unable to hold her feeling, and day by day I grew in fear of what was coming of this sorrowful coil.

Sir Hugh drank none the less for his kinsman's presence, and it was on a day as he sat dozing in the hall beside his empty flagon that Godfrey and my lady played at chess in the embrasure of the window. I sat apart, laying in color on a missal which I was illuminating for my lady's own oratory. Since Marian's prating my lady strove ever to keep me anear her when Godfrey was within the Manor. Though 't was but a thankless task to play the bulwark which dammed up her flowing love for another, yet, withal, I rejoiced to be even so much of worth to her.

Godfrey was for trapping my lady into acknowledgment that she still bore love to him. Quoth he: "I pray thee give me thy counsel, fair kinswoman. I have a companion in arms, one most dear to me, who loved a damsel beyond measure. She gave her heart to his keeping — or so she did profess — and pledged her to await his coming from the Holy Wars. Now that he is returned, he doth find her wedded with another who hath land and gold. I besought him forget the faithless jade, but thou being a woman may discern her action in a something different light. What wouldst thou say to my comrade an thou spake with him?"

My lady leaned her cheek in her hand; keeping her eyes fixed on the chess pieces, she did seem to ruminate of her next move. The sun through the stained window turned her hair to a great glory. Her right hand was above the board as a hovering bird. Saith she, at length, moving her piece with deliberateness:

"Thou hast given thy friend wise counsel, to which I would add nor take aught. Bid him forget the jade." Then saith she, in quiet tone, "Check."

Silence lasted while he did extricate his piece from its threatened position, then saith he again: "Something there is which doth change the complexion of the affair I spoke on. The man to whom the damsel is wedded is no true knight, but a base-bred coward who would flee his shadow at noonday an it bore a lance. Beside the which, he be drunken and ribald: bethink you, doth not this something alter the matter?"

Again her hand slow hovered o'er the board. "I be loth to think that a gentlman of name, arms, and cry, could be as thou dost depict, noble cousin. Zeal for thy friend hath colored thy vision." Then saith she again, "Check."

"By St. Christopher, my lady, I swear I have but touched in the picture gray, an it were rightly black, which being so, dost thou not deem my comrade hath warrant to bear his love from the churl to a place of safety and defy her lord to combat *à l'outrance?*" quoth he, and he did make a hasty move.

"Nay, but dost thou not think thy comrade something presumptuous to thus assume that the damsel still careth for him? Beshrew me, it hath that look to me," then saith she, and she did make another move — "Checkmate." By which I knew that my lady had won the game.

At this his blue eyes cast upon her such a grieving look of reproach for that she had seemed to so deny her love for him, she scarce could bear the sight. She paled under his glance and did even impulsive start, as though to throw aside the game she had but now won and own herself weak and defeated. Full well I knew the words of tenderness that were crowding to her lips, — for it were mistake to deem my lady cold, that she was not, — and being quickly aware an I would save her that for which she would ne'er hold herself forgiven, with ruthless hand I swept from my desk a pot of crimson pigment. It fell, sounding loudly on the tense silence of the room, dashing a stain like blood across the floor. The sleeping drunkard stirred to grumbling movement, straightly settling to sleep again. Nor my lady, nor Godfrey, so much as turned their heads; nathless I saw that the sudden sound had loosed her fascinated gaze, which 'til now had been holden to Godfrey's by a power stronger than herself.

Rising quickly from her place she stood over against him, tall and fair, gazing at him with darkening eyes which did at once command and plead to him.

"Godfrey, it were inhospitable to speak thus, I wis, but why tarriest thou at Weregrave? The king who set forward on his journey from Palestine before thy leaving is not yet come to England. Some say him dead; others, that he lies captive in the hands of his foes. Prince John's hand already closes over the sceptre, and thou, loyal knight to so great a master, bidest here in springtime idleness when every true subject should be stirring."

At this the blood came with a mighty rush in Godfrey's face, and the little scar 'neath his eye burned to a deep color. He made answer in tone so low I scarce could catch his utterance.

"Thou art ever right, my lady, and I am recreant knight." Then, forgetful of my presence, or that of the sleeping drunkard, he broke out in passionate entreaty, "How can I go hence, how tear me from Weregrave an thou loose not first the jesses which bind my heart to thy hand?" and he did gaze upon her with a look it well-nigh broke her heart to deny.

"Say not 't is I that hold thee," she pled with him, "I bid thee go. Honor and service are still thine; be not unworthy these, I beseech thee."

"Say rather, sweet, be not unworthy thee," saith he, bending his head as he were in a holy place.

On the morrow he took horse and departed. Nor in word or look did he aught to vex my lady again; and, womanlike, I do believe she felt herself despitefully used withal, in that he had not let his eyes say that which she forbade his lips to utter.

Life at Weregrave settled to its wonted heaviness after this. My lady showed no grief, an she felt any, at Godfrey's going. I do bethink me so much of sorrow had numbed her sense and dulled the sharpness of her feeling.

Sir Hugh's potations were daily deeper, and he grew ever in cothyness. Seldom rode he now to hunt or hawk, contenting him with the fireside and his brimming flagon.

Now hath my tale brought me to that on which I would I could hold silence. This may not be, nor can I of honesty keep back mine own guiltiness, in those things which befell us.

Well do I know that though the act was another's, my hand doth wear on it a guilty stain, in that I might have hindered a wrong and did not. And this be not the most grievous part of the matter, withal, for though I am ware that sin lieth on my soul, yet am I not sorrowful of the act which put it there, nor can I bring myself to be. Doubtless in another world I will burn for this, it scarce could be otherwise; but when I recall how much of joy hath come through it for my lady, I can but say, 'twere worth the damnation of one such poor soul as mine to have it thus.

But to my tale, for as yet thou knowest naught of the happenings of which I speak.

'T is one of my tasks at Weregrave, being almoner, to give each morn from the Manor gate the dole of food and trenchers from my lord's table to the beggars who come hither.

For three morns I had beheld 'mongst the clamoring crowd one who looked of better sort despite that his clothing was rent and grimed and his visage hollow as any. Within his great eyes there lurked the look as a famished wolf who scents prey. Notwithstanding, he made no move to take of the proffered food, and when I had thought thereon it seemed to me he must be a witless one.

So thinking, on the fourth morn of his coming

I pressed aside the rude horde of more importunate ones and of myself thrust into his hand a well-sopped trencher of bread. Scarce had his fingers touched it than he unclasped them and let fall upon the dusty road the tasty bit. Quick as thought two lusty fellows fell on it, but ere their greedy clutch had fastened thereon, the beggar set foot squarely on the bread and ground it into the dirt.

"How now, sirrah," quoth I, angered at such wantonness, "is it thus you treat my lord's bounty? Get you gone ere I have you beaten from the gate."

Whereupon the beggar turned upon me a look which was like a knife in the body. "'T is not my lord's bread that I crave, but his blood," quoth he, and saying this straight lost himself in the crowd and passed from my sight ere I could stay him.

Much I pondered on this happening and what it did portend, but naught of it did I utter to Sir Hugh, for that he would have had his varlets scour the countryside 'til they found the fellow and beat the life o' him.

Some half a score of days after, or perchance it was a two weeks, — of this point I hold no certainty, but this I do know, 't was the hour of tierce and we sat at meat, while a fierce storm brewed without. The wind roared and howled in the chimney as a soul in the pit, and darkness was come on so thick that the torches were perforce lit in the hall. My lord paled and shivered at each blast which howled over the Manor, — he seeming ever craven when storms broke heavy. Of a truth, much liquor had brought him to a state of such jumping fright the least sound was like to well-nigh scare him from his body.

In the midst of this tempest there came at the gate a blind beggar craving shelter; who, when he was come within the hall, dripping and miserable, my lady, ever pitiful, bade Marian lead him anear the fire and there serve him with food. Thereupon Marian did set before him a trencher steaming with savory meat, which he seemed not to heed, hovering 'gainst the fire, shivering and shivering, 'til I counted him a poor witless fool as well as blind. Something of familiarity there wās about the man, though I could not say in what it lay. Once I was for fancying I had glimpsed a sight of a pair of hungry wolfish eyes gleaming 'neath his dirty head-covering.

When dinner was at an end Sir Hugh made as if to cross the hall, and I, I scarce know why, followed in haste. I know not if 't were accident or design, but the beggar moved from the fireside and stood in my lord's way; at which, being roundly drunk, he kicked the poor creature from him with a mighty oath. I saw the man straighten himself, I saw the gleam of uplifted steel, and quick as the fellow moved, I had yet been quick enough to stay his hand had I so willed. But I did not. 'T was life and freedom for my lady which I saw in the gleam of that upraised knife. While I thought thus, I saw the steel strike home to Sir Hugh's breast.

"Take that, and that, and that!" shouted the beggar, "and I would I could strike thee once for every pang which she hath suffered of thee, for then would thy body be one gaping wound."

Sir Hugh fell, the blood gushing from half a score of holes, the man atop of him using his knife to awful purpose.

When my lord's men had gathered their wit and did attempt to take the murderer, he stood at bay, threatening all with his knife. His head uplifted, I saw 't was the same who had spurned my lord's bounty at the gate, as I did tell thee on.

"Lay no hand on me," he cried in frenzy; "he died justly. He came a-hunting near my hut; he saw my child, my only one; he used her to his wicked will; for that he lies weltering in his blood," — and before any could stay the mad creature, he had turned his knife 'gainst himself, severing the great vein in his neck, which spurted forth like a fountain of red. Then fell he forward over Sir Hugh's corpse, and the blood of knight and villain, oppressor and oppressed, mingled and crimsoned the rushes on the floor.

For a brief space my lady stood over this

awful sight, white and solemn; then raising her hand on high, saith she:

"This justice was from heaven. Your lord died by the hand of God."

Of Sir Hugh's funeral and the long feasting, wherein wine and ale flowed like water, and every sort from beggar to lord caroused at Weregrave, I will say naught. My lady kept her chamber, permitting none to see her; not that she felt grief or made pretence thereof, for this she did not. In all things she had outward respect to the name she bore, and bade me see to it that every ceremony was faithfully observed. One thing she would not, however, — that Sir Hugh be buried at Weregrave.

"The men of our blood and lineage," saith she " have ever borne themselves as brave knights and true men. 'T were insult to their dust that such an one be laid amongst them."

So when the hour of sepulture was come, Sir Hugh was borne to Hardecute Castle, and there left in the vault 'neath the chapel altar.

Beside this, my lady bade me see to it that the body of the poor villain have decent burial, and once when I spake on him as murderer, she chid me soundly.

"Nay, Anselm, never call the deed murder; 't was execution." Which, heaven be my witness, I think it was.

All this being over and done, Weregrave settled to a calm so great 't was nigh to the peace of heaven, and had it not been for my lady's failing looks and drooping figure, I had a'most thought me transported to another world.

With her, 't was as if a tight-strung bow had on a sudden snapped its string. Scarce could you say that she ailed, for that she did not, nor would she drink Marian's brews and possets which the faithful wench had ever ready to thrust 'neath her nose an she cough, or sneeze, or sigh. But all the lightsomeness was gone from out her step, and for hours together would she sit, with idle hands folded and eyes wide apart, seeing naught in this world, I am fain to believe.

Oft we tarried in the garden court on the sundial seat where first I beheld her grieving over her sorry fate. Her weary head would she rest 'gainst the dial, while sun-kissed, and bird songs lulled her to quiet. Sometimes would I read to her from a romaunt, or recite to her the lay of some minstrel. I know not if her outward ears gave heed to the words which I uttered, but the drone of my voice seemed pleasing to her sense, and my presence, at least, not distasteful, and so I was content.

Once as we sat thus, she of her own will harked back to the hour of our meeting here, which thing she had never so much as spoken on afore. "Dost thou mind, Anselm," quoth she, "how thou didst say to me that Time healed all wounds? 'Tis a wise saying if something old, but I am given to doubt if it be true. Time can scarce wipe away the assoil of some things."

I was silent, for I knew that she did speak of her life with Sir Hugh, and of a truth 'twas a hard matter for forgetting.

Thus the days of peace slipped by, and each morn would I say within myself, "This will be the last, for to-day Godfrey will come;" and each night would I add one more day to the string of which memory did make a rosary, and tell over hour by hour with joy.

Still Godfrey came not, and Marian began to say with openness, when my lady was not near, "He hath forgot." My lady's drooping mien, I fear, did utter the same, "He hath forgot;" and within mine own heart, a whisper, half sorrowful, wholly joyful, said also, "He hath forgot."

I know not why it was that I so dreaded Godfrey's coming, — Godfrey whom I ever loved as my own soul; but of a truth I did so dread it, it seeming to me that his coming must change all things and perchance bring pain within our walls again.

'Twas at this time that one, a knight, Reginald Beauvais, rode from London to the provinces and stopped the night at Weregrave; who being come from the court, was stuffed to the throat with gossip thereof, and bore to us the first tidings of Godfrey which we had had of him since his riding from Weregrave.

In the unfolding of his budget, he recounted to us how after much hardship and shameful imprisoning — which 't was more than guessed the forsworn Philip of France had a thumb in — that Richard was at length returned to England, and how that Godfrey was in great favor of the monarch because of having twice rescued him from death in Palestine. But further he went on to relate that this favor was little like to be of service to him, for that 't was public rumor that Godfrey lay grievously sick of a fever and like to die thereof.

"Of a truth," saith he with a careless lightness ill becoming to any, though doubtless but the foppish fashion of the town, where all things, or life, or death, are to be borne lightly, "he is most like a'ready dead, for none who knew of his malady had hope to his life."

At this I saw my lady turn as white as the cloth which covered the board, — we being at meat the while, — and I feared the sudden evil news had wholly undone her. Howbeit, she struggled mightily to hold her grief, and bore herself with quiet 'til the meal was ended. I plied the youth with many questions of Godfrey and his whereabouts in the town, being minded to ride thence on the morrow if my lady allow. But for this was I not prepared, that my lady should take it to her head to ride to London also.

Marian came straightly to fetch me to my

lady's chamber so soon as our guest was retired, and there I found Joscelyn pacing the floor as a wild creature, her long calm broken at last. Again had the master hand set string to the bow and tightened it with the winch. Fearfully I watched her, deeming her strength too frail and spent to withstand so sudden a strain. With no loss of time she unfolded her design to me in speech so hurried that her words did jostle one another as rude fellows, each with his toe on another's heel.

When she had made an end of speaking I pled long with her that she suffer me to go alone, pledging her to do all that mortal might for Godfrey's mending, and when he was himself once more, to fetch him straight to Weregrave. I represented to her that she was not in health for such heavy undertaking as this hard journey to London.

To all she turned deaf ear, or met me with a counter plea so melting, that I had worn a most monstrous hard heart an I yielded not; as I presently did.

Then was I for coaxing her that she proceed to Winchester, ten miles distant, and from thence to the coast, there to take ship for London; the journey thus being accomplished with greater ease if longer time.

"Nay, Anselm, trammel me not in this. If I do go as thou art minded to have, we must needs wait the sailing of a ship, besides putting ourselves at the mercy, it may perchance be, of an adverse wind. The weariness of a journey were not so great as would be the eating o' my heart with impatience. Every day, ay, every hour, doth count a lifetime now. We will set forward on the morrow at nones, and thus be able to come easily to Winchester ere night falls and the gates be shut. There will we lay the night and be well rested for beginning our hard journey. I implore thee say no more. It shall be thus."

And so it was, my lady having her will in this as in all things. The next day at nones, after most hasty preparation, we set forward for Winchester. My lady, mounted on her white mule and arrayed in a gown of deep green stuff laced with gold, wore a flush of excitement on her cheek which well-nigh tricked one to believe it the sign of returning health. Beside her rode Marian in a mighty state of intrancement for that she journeyed to London for the first time of her life. With us went twenty-five of our stoutest men-at-arms, well provided with weapons; for the roads are beset with thieves and cutpurses who lay in wait for travellers of the better sort; it being mightily unsafe to strive to reach London an we go not well guarded. A host of serving people rode with us as well, for, as thou art ware, after passing Winchester there be no hospitable monasteries wherein we may lay the night, and the inns be not fit place for any save tavern brawlers and such low sort.

The tinkle, tinkle, tinkle of the silver bells upon my lady's bridle sounded forth riotously at our starting, seeming to my fancy like joy-bells; but ere we were come within sight of the monastery towers at Winchester my lady drooped right wearily in her saddle, while the bridle, lying lax on the mule's neck, no longer stirred the bells to brave music. I dare be sworn she was not a little glad when we rode within the gate-house of the monastery.

Here, in the guest-house, shortly after our coming, was arrayed for us a supper consisting of not a few dishes quaint and new to our taste, over which Marian had a mighty curiosity; and here we reposed the night in comfort.

On the morrow, ere we took horse, my lady bade me give, over and above the sum wherewith to settle our reckoning, a pound sterling for masses to be said for Godfrey's recovery. And never in our journeying did she pass a rude cross or wayside shrine an she did not pause to put up a prayer for him she so loved. I think it did hurt her sore to remember that whilst he lay a-dying she was for doubting his loyalty.

Before the ending of the first day of our leaving Winchester, my lady was well-nigh falling from her saddle in utter weariness. The serving people had pressed on before us some hours earlier, and had raised a tent for the women. As we rode up to the spot, the camp-fires blazed brightly. In the waning light I could see the cook and scullions busily engaged in making ready for our evening meal. A savory odor of pottage floated to my nose, whetting my already keen appetite to an edge 'twas like to take a mighty bowl of the stuff to dull.

My lady was so spent with fatigue I needs must lift her from her mule and bear her straight to the couch already waiting her; this I did, my heart gripping me the while with a fierce pain I know not how to word, for that her weight seemed so slight a thing even for my poor strength.

When the supper was made ready Marian knelt beside the couch on which my lady reclined and coaxed her to each mouthful with the pretty fooling which women use toward an ailing child. Nathless, despite her coaxing, and my lady's striving, 'twas little enough of the strengthening stuff she took, and Marian shook her head sadly, gazing into the bowl still so nearly full.

But as we drew anear to our journey's end, my lady grew stronger, despite the fatigue, till at length, at the end of the fourth day of our starting, we came in sight of London town.

Here we tarried without the gate to crave shelter for the night at the Benedictine nunnery of St. John the Baptist for my lady and Marian; it being ill fit that they stay the night at a tavern, and I, scarce knowing where to command lodging for them of any of the burgher class, being so much a stranger to the town.

When I had seen them safe bestowed for the night, I took my way within the city, none too soon an I did not desire to have the gates closed 'gainst me; not, however, 'til I had promised my lady to return for her in the morn so soon as light was come.

I sought out a quiet inn in a narrow street where I had lodged on the only time of my being in London, and having seen to it with mine own eyes that the animals were well housed and fed, and our men-at-arms reasonably disposed for the night, I made the best I could of some unsavory viands and got me to my couch, full of weariness. Despite my great weariness, however, 'twas not to sleep, for notwithstanding this tavern is counted a sober spot and quiet, 'twas the unheard-of time of a two hours beyond compline ere the noise of the inn gave place to quiet.

So soon as the city gates were open on the morrow, I with two serving men fared forth to the nunnery for my lady and Marian. Early as I was, my lady was waiting me with fretting impatience.

Her looks were pale, and great circles of dark blue lay 'neath her eyes, giving them a look of monstrous size. I was fearful that the journey had borne too greatly on her strength, and said as much as we rode along. Whereat she shook her head, answering,—

"'Tis not the journey which hath worn so upon me, but through all the night I tossed upon my couch nor closed mine eyes for thinking of Godfrey within the near-by city, perchance a-dying, and thou wouldst not let me seek him."

"Speak not thus, my lady, I beseech you," prayed I, mightily cut at her words. "I did but act in this as seemed wisest for thee. 'T was nightfall ere we ourselves were housed at the inn; had we sought Godfrey on the hour as thou wert for doing, it had been a'ready black night ere we reached his abode. Thou art ware that after nightfall the city streets are infested with a brawling and factious sort, who but seek occasion in a quarrel to run thee through the body, and so have opportunity to relieve thee of thy purse. Beside the which I know not how Dame Bardulf, with whom Godfrey hath lodging, is situate, or if she be able to command proper lodging for thee. Say that I did aright, my lady. It grieves me sorely to be under even slight blame of thee."

Whereon, as ever it is her gentle custom, she soothed the hurt she had unwitting wrought. Thus we proceeded through the city, nor did any of its sights or sounds, so unwonted to our country-bred eyes and ears, seem to have even slight notice of her, so intent was she on thoughts of Godfrey; though Marian was like to wring her head from her shoulders in her desire to lose no whit of it all.

On our way we passed through Chepe, which word is a Saxon one and signifies Market. Only the south side of this way is built upon, the north of it being an open field where jousts, tourneys or ridings are often held. The houses along this way be monstrous fine, and many goldsmith and linendrapers there keep shop.

Here it was that we passed a crowd of people of the commoner sort, who stood about the pillory where a scurvy knave of a baker was fastened, a gazing stock to all; his offence being that he had made his loaves something light of weight for honesty.

At length were we come to a street called Watling, and having proceeded some distance thereon I did espy, hung from a pole, a sign bearing this inscription: "Simon Bardulf, Pepperer," which being the direction given me by the knight, Reginald Beauvais, I knew we were come at length to our journey's end.

We drew rein before the shop, where a rosy-faced prentice boy kept the air in motion with a voice whose rasping cry must needs gain him the ear of each passer-by. "What d' ye lack, what d' ye lack, what d' ye lack?"

Upon inquiring of the youth if Dame Bardulf was within, he paused of his cry long enough to answer:

"Of that I know not, see you, but I dare be sworn she is, for she seldom fares forth at this hour. My master hath to the guild-hall of

Pepperers this morn on great business, and I do tend shop in his place. Most worshipful sir, can I serve you in aught?"

"In naught save direction of where to find thy mistress," quoth I, nothing pleased at the youth's pert tongue.

"Down the passage to the right, and up the stairs. There knock loudly, for the Dame hath one ear deaf, though, by my faith, the other is ever for taking account of that which it is not intended she should."

Helping my lady to alight, we took our way through a narrow passage, followed now loudly, then dimly, by the prentice's rasping call, 'til we found ourselves in a great square court in the midst of which stood a well-house whence all the burghers on the court drew water. From this court many flights of stone stairs led to the upper story.

Turning into the nearest of these we ascended, and stood before a heavy oaken door.

Remembering the advice of the malapert prentice, I delivered a heavy knock on the portal.

On the instant it was flung wide by an angry hand, and there appeared within the opening a goodwife, short and fat, whose round red face had a look of kindly good nature, despite that now it did show anger at my untoward summons.

"How now, sirrah?" she was beginning, when, seeing by my dress and bearing that I was other than she expected, she did modify her tone greatly. "I cry you pardon, good sir; I was for basting thee soundly, deeming thee one of those malapert prentices who will have the life o' me yet with their tormenting—"

"Yes, yes, good woman, but I would hold speech with Dame Bardulf," saith I, seeing I must stem the torrent of her speech ere it o'erflow me.

"Then say thy say, sir, for thou dost hold speech with her this instant." Whereupon, glimpsing my lady, who 'til now had been hidden by me, on a sudden the Dame's manner changed. For there is that in Joscelyn's bearing which, an she be alone or unattended, will ever make a common person bend to her. Straight the woman stood aside, begging us enter and honor her poor abode by being seated.

Quoth my lady, "Good Dame Bardulf, we seek one Godfrey de Bersac, a knight who hath, if I mistake not, had lodging of thee this long time. It hath come to us, his kinspeople, that he lieth grievously sick of a fever, and we have ridden far to help recover him of his illness."

Hearing this, the good Dame threw her kirtle over her head and 'gan to rock herself and weep in such fashion that my lady went pale as a spirit and was like to drop.

"Nay, never tell me that we are too late, that he is a'ready dead," she moaned, grasping the woman's kirtle in her hand and clinging to it pitifully.

"Ah, body o' me, body o' me, if it were no worse!" exclaimed the Dame, still rocking her body and weeping, "though for any knowledge that be mine he may be that beside. And of a truth 'twere better so, than to rot o' a prison."

"Woman, of your mercy unfold this matter to my hearing. Is not the knight here with thee, and if not what hath befallen him, where hath he gone?" quoth my lady, her tone fraught with fear and anguish.

"That may your worships well ask o' me. An I were God or the king I might answer thee. Look you, my lady, 'twas on this wise he went hence. Many weeks agone the youth fell on sickness, and did burn of a fever, the which I never saw the like on afore, so great was it. In the twinkling of an eye, as a body might say, he was raving and out of himself. I perforce must fight him an I keep him to his bed; for he was ever for mounting his destrier and riding to a place I know not on, but which he often named in his madness, called Weregrave. He who was ever of such gentle way toward all that never heard I ill word of him, would now contend 'gainst me with mad strength, pummelling me in such sound manner that I oft must call the prentice boys of my good man an I keep the youth to his bed.

"Oh, I did give him gentle care, my lady, I promise you that, for he ever used kindness toward me. Down his throat I did pour divers brews and possets — of which I have great skill in the preparation — he being out of himself, as a body might say, and not able to withstand me. For of a truth, had he been other, I had never ha' gotten a one of them i' the inside o' him, he liking such stuff not a whit.

"The barber-surgeon was summoned, and did come day on day and bleed him, 'til belike the poor creature's blood was well-nigh drained of him, and yet he did not mend."

"Of thy goodness, Dame, get thee to the end of this and let me have knowledge of what hath befallen him," quoth my lady, sore tried at listening to the woman's ceaseless chatter of possets and brews and bleedings when she yet knew not if Godfrey were live or dead.

"Ay, ay, your worship, I come to that now. Thou shouldst not blame me because that my tongue cannot keep pace with thy chafing impatience. 'T is a fault o' heaven's making and hath ever been said of me — and Simon my husband doth lay it greatly to my credit — that I be never one to talk much, or as a body might say, to talk fast. In these days of scolds and chatters, my lady, 't were no defect to be of a silent turn, I do beg thee know," quoth the Dame, pouring out the words so fast that they did seem an endless stream, never to be stayed or dammed.

My lady seeing that she must be wary, an she

turn aside all this and gain of the woman the answer she longed to hear, saith most gently now, but I could hear the impatience beneath her soft tone:

"Ay, good Dame, thou hast the right of it in this; but thou wert for telling me, when I so unmannerly interrupted thee, where they bore Sir Godfrey an they took him hence."

"Nay, my lady, not so, for that I could not; and grief for this hath so wrought upon me this two weeks, I scarce have eaten a gobbet and am falling to a shadow o' myself; so Simon, my master, did say to me only this morn. Of a truth 't is little wonder that I sorrow thus, for the knight was of such gentle sort, and ready was he to the day with his lodge money, to which he ever added a little sum for fairings. 'T is not oft in these times that one finds such, beshrew me, so when they took him hence, I was for fighting as a wolf doth for her whelps. But what could I, my lady, when I beheld the king's own seal?"

"Naught, good Dame, save that which thou didst, I am persuaded. But thou sayest it was at the king's command that he was borne hence?" questioned my lady, fearful that she again turn aside the Dame in her speech.

"Of that I know not, my lady, save that a soldier read the parchment to me and pointed out a round red thing not greatly smaller than a bun, which he did aver was the king's own seal. 'T was on this wise that they came for him. As to-day, one gave a sounding knock on the portal, and when I was come to open it, meaning to give the knave a piece of my tongue for that he had disturbed my patient, I beheld at my threshold not a few of the king's soldiers, who bore amongst them a litter. They thrust me aside most churlishly when I had opened to them, demanding in no mannerly tone that I point out to them where lay the knight Godfrey de Bersac; and when I would not, but desired to know their business, they told me they were come to bear him hence. 'Nay, that you will not,' quoth I, right roundly; 'the man hath little of life in him now, and I will not that it be shaken out of him at thy villain hands.' Whereon one drew forth from his pouch the parchment I spoke on bearing the king's seal, which, according to his reading, did say I was to deliver into the hands of the bearers the body of Godfrey de Bersac, be he live or dead. Upon this I fell a-crying, and begged them tell me of what crime he stood accused and to what place they would fetch him. But to this they gave no heed, and one chucked me 'neath the chin in most unmannerly fashion and bade me have no fear, for that they would bed him comfortably in a cool dungeon, where the fever of him would cool swiftly enough, and rats and toads act right gentle nurses to him; whereat I 'gan to wail afresh, while they lifted his poor body from the couch — right gently I will say — and laid him in the litter and bore him I know not where. I essayed to follow them and find out, when one lusty fellow turned back and drove me home at the point of his pike, I a-shrieking with fright at each step and feeling that sharp weapon in my buttocks."

After questioning the Dame closely and finding that we could draw from her no further knowledge, for that she had none, we were forced to depart and leave her standing by the roadside where she had followed us, still chattering and protesting that no fault lay with her in this matter and calling all the saints to witness of her sorrow.

I would then that my lady return to the convent and there await me while I made search of the town for my brother, of whose fate I now held deep fears which I dared not word to her. But to this she said me a right round nay, and bade me turn on the instant toward the Tower. "For," saith she, "an he be taken prisoner for some invented offence, 'tis there he most like is."

'Twas no great way from the lodging of Dame Bardulf to where we would go, but being strange to it we were forced to ask our way of burgher and shopman 'til at length we found ourselves before the Tower. About it lies a deep moat inclosing a double line of fortifications, from the centre of which doth rise a monstrous great quadrangular tower having a turret at each corner thereof. Having passed the drawbridge, the portcullis was drawn up, and we were let to enter after some delay. Once within the great court, I made demand of the fellow who admitted us that we be straightly led into the presence of the governor of the Tower, with whom I had important business. The knave did lay great hindrance in our way, and was for refusing our request outright despite that he did see that we were people of some sorts. 'T was not 'til I named myself the brother of Sir Godfrey de Bersac that he gave heed to my request.

"Nay, if thou hadst but named that to me in the beginning," quoth he, becoming on a sudden monstrous obliging, "I had not stayed thee;" and he straight led us into a great hall, which is a portion of the governor's apartments and where the governor himself shortly joined us.

I lost no time in unfolding our tale and begging of him that he first tell me of what my brother stood accused, and then of his goodness permit me to hold converse with him.

As I talked I saw grow within the man's face a look of amaze; ere I had made an end of speaking he broke forth:

"This tale which thou dost bring me is passing strange, Sir Anselm, for thy brother stands accused of no crime that I wot of, nor have I knowledge of where he lieth save only this, that 't is not within the Tower of London. It doth rather wear the look to me of some private vengeance; perchance he hath been foully dealt with. But an it come to King Richard's ear that any hath done him despite, beshrew me, I would have little relish for standing in the fellow's shoes."

At hearing such dire forebodings from the governor's lips my lady's frail strength forsook her; she had fallen to the floor, an I had not caught her and borne her to a near-by settle, where she reclined, looking for all that I could see as one dead. After a time, with much care from Marian, who chafed her hands and burned not a few goosequills beneath her nose — the faithful wench having fetched a pocket full of them lest some such thing befall — my lady recovered herself, and was for pushing on without delay to Westminster Palace where the king was, desiring to lay our grievance at his feet without the smallest delay. 'Twas vain that I did urge upon her her unfitness for greater fatigue — that the Palace was a full league and a half distant; that the hour of tierce was long passed, while her fast remained unbroken since morn. She set aside my words with a gesture which bade me be silent, and walked from the hall bearing herself with more of steadiness than I deemed her capable.

The governor, being much touched by her beauty and distress, perchance fearful as well that suspicion might rest upon him in the matter — for that the Dame did maintain that it was the king's soldier who had borne Godfrey from his lodging — proffered his service to ride with us to the king, which offer we right gladly accepted.

Thus for a third time that morn we set out in search of Godfrey, and each time hope was become weaker within us.

The whole of our way to the Palace lay now beside the river Thames, where we saw not a few monstrous great ships from distant lands. For, as the governor of the Tower did point out to us with much pride, London was now become a mighty mart, and commerce was come to her from every part of the earth.

At length, after a weary way of riding for my lady, we were come in sight of an incomparable structure furnished with a breastwork and bastion, which I knew on the instant to be the king's palace, having once before beheld it.

Here, after not a little of formality, we were ushered into an ante-room to await while the message that the governor of the Tower craved audience with the king passed from guard to page, from page to gentleman-in-waiting, 'til it reach the king's ear.

The room in which we waited was a marvel of beauty to my country sight, having about the wall a wondrously wrought arras into which had been sewn a marvellous great picture of a hawking party. Over the floor was spread a cloth of such richness and thickness that our footsteps melted into its depth and were lost to sound. The seats were a very miracle of the cutter's art. The portal at the end of this room gave on a pair of steps which led down to the king's own pleasure garden, where flowers, the gayest and most rare, flaunted in the sunshine, and winding walks led hither and yon. All these things I could not fail to note while we waited; though so far as my lady was concerned these sights fell on blinded eyes. I dare be sworn that Marian missed no whit of it all, for there she sat, fearsomely quiet, with eyes so agog of amaze that 'twas great wonder they did not roll from her silly head and leave her forever blinded.

The minutes dragged wearily. My lady sat breathing as a spent runner, with fixed gaze fastened upon the portal through which the messenger had passed, for all the world as she were witched and not able to withdraw her eyes from the spot. I could see that the pink of her finger-nails was become white from the pressure of her tight-clasped hands, and I knew that to her, seconds were now become hours.

At length a page came down the corridor, and, pausing at the entrance, informed us that his majesty was at this time engaged, and if the governor would see him, he must wait the morrow, when the king would give him audience at the hour of nones.

Then outspake the governor, "Go you again to his majesty; say to him that my business is of greatest urgence, and beg him of his goodness that he see me without delay."

"Nay, that I will not, my lord Governor. When the king hath given a nay, he likes not to be importuned," quoth the page.

"Nathless, I bid thee go again, good youth," saith my lady, now rising and going to the lad, upon whose arm she laid her soft compelling touch. "Say to him that 't is for the welfare of Godfrey de Bersac that he hear me. Say to him that the knight's brother and kinswoman have ridden from beyond the good city of Winchester to seek Sir Godfrey, who, 't was said, lay a-dying of a fever. Say that when we were come, 't was to find him gone from his lodgings, none knew whither; say all this, nay, even more, add thy prayers to mine, as thou hast hope some day to be true knight," pleaded my lady, her great eyes soft with unfallen tears. The lad gazed spellbound upon her, with that look which her beauty ever calls forth from high or low, or youth or age.

"By my faith, hadst thou informed me sooner that 't was in the name of de Bersac that thou craved audience with the king, thou hadst not been thus shortly set aside; but now I beg thee know, fair maid, an the king speaks a nay, one may not lightly ask of him again. Beside the which, he hath even now gone forth into the plaisance with some of the court. Beshrew me, there he comes but now," and the lad pointed through the window to a group who moved along one of the walks.

For the first time of my life I beheld Richard of England. Walking in advance of the others, his hand lightly resting on the arm of my lord Percy, methinks never before or since have I beheld the like for strength and bodily beauty. He walked unbonneted, seeming to joy in the rays of the warm sun; his red-gold hair just touched his shoulders, its ends soft curling of their own will; his face had cast off its prison paleness and now glowed with ruddy health. He was habited in a robe of blue, richly sewn with a powdering of gold stitchery.

While I gazed upon him, lost in admiring, my lady had passed swiftly to the oaken door which gave on the stair leading to the plaisance, and ere I was ware of her intent, or could raise hand to stay her, she had passed out of the portal, down the stairs, and was a'ready kneeling at the feet of the king, who had paused in amaze, doubtless thinking her some apparition sprung from the ground at his feet, so sudden was her coming.

The king's face wore a slight frown an he gazed upon her, for he likes not to be interrupted in his pleasuring. Marian had pushed herself without the portal, and now stood at my side shaking and chattering with fright, gasping as a fish drawn from water. I do believe the silly wench was for thinking that the king would straightly draw his sword and strike off my lady's head without more ado, because of her temerity in thus going unbidden into his presence.

"How now, lady, what do you here? Is it that the monarch can claim no moment to himself without some suppliant at his feet to importune him?" he questioned with something of anger in his tone.

"Justice, your majesty, I crave justice for one of your loyal servants," saith she, raising her face and disclosing its beauty and sorrow to the king's gaze. I could hear a little murmuring of admiration pass amongst the courtiers who stood back, and, so potent is a fair face, even the king's brow cleared of its frown. He stretched forth his hand to her, saying the while:

"Rise, lady, I command thee; it were not meet that so much of beauty should be at the feet of any man."

My lady only lifted her wondrous eyes and fastened them on the king's face with a glance of pain and supplication in their depths. Quoth she, scarce able to restrain her tears for fright and sorrow, "My liege, I kneel before thee to beg at thy hands justice for thy loyal knight and loving servant, Godfrey de Bersac, who, it beseemeth, hath been foully dealt with by some villain enemy; unless it be true that at his majesty's command Godfrey hath been thrown into prison; though God wot of what crime he could be charged. Not 'gainst thee, my lord king, for he did ever love thee as his own soul, nor 'gainst thy law, for to it he gave submissive heed. Of thy mercy, then, I beseech thee, say what hath befallen him an thou knowest."

"Of one thing be assured, lady, Godfrey de Bersac stands accused of no crime 'gainst king or state; nor at our command hath he been cast into prison. As soon would I cut my right hand from me as doubt the loyalty of him who twice put his life in jeopardy that his king might go free. He who wears the motto, 'Je suis le Roi,' is too much king to be traitor. But I pray thee unfold to my hearing what relation thou bearest to this same knight." And despite that the king held a solemn tone I saw a smile of whimsey come in his eyes as he had but now heard somewhat which did mightily amuse him. Calling a page to him, he delivered a low-toned command to the youth, who quickly departed through a door which led into the Palace.

Upon this Joscelyn went mightily red, but answered bravely, notwithstanding:

"Sire, ere he rode to Palestine, I was his betrothed, but my father of his wisdom forced me wed with another, who being now dead, I am again free to love as I would."

"And if I should say to thee that Godfrey hath tired of his long waiting, and given his love to another, a damsel of the court who hath great store of gold, what wouldst thou then?" quoth the king, with the look of whimsey still in his eyes.

My lady was on her feet i' the instant, with head held aloft. She looked at the king a long minute, and I did see a jealous distrust and high-mettled pride creep within her eyes and straighten the curve of her perfect mouth. It was passed a'most as soon as come, and in its place a tender smile of memory came to her lips. "Then," quoth she right boldly, and my lady upheld her head and gazed upon the king with eyes like shining stars, "would I answer thee, despite that a king hath uttered it, 'twere false, for Godfrey's heart lies ever in my keeping."

"By all the saints, that were nobly spoken, my lady, and thou art well deserving the love of such an one as Godfrey de Bersac. And I do here pledge thee our royal word to seek out the villain enemy of whom thou spakest, and if thou dost find the knight harmed in body or purse, or thyself holding aught 'gainst the fellow who has thus taken him by force, I will see to it that he be soundly punished, and thou thyself shalt set the penalty."

Scarcely had the king ceased to utter this promise in solemn tone, but with a twinkling eye which gave me to doubt an he were as ignorant of Godfrey's whereabouts as he made appearance of, than shuffling footsteps sounded at the door by which the page had gone. Suddenly was it thrown open, and we beheld Godfrey, weak and pale, leaning on the stalwart shoulders of two lusty fellows.

"My love, my lady," cried he, forgetful of king or courtiers, of all save her whom he so dearly loved. Making a weak step toward her he fell kneeling at her feet.

With a cry which seemed to compass all of love in its sound, for it held a maid's love for her lover, a wife's love to her lord, and a mother's for her best-loved child, she gathered Godfrey's head within her arms and bent her lips to his.

A long minute they stayed thus, forgetful of all save that they were at length together after weary months of separation. The salt water was come to mine eyes with a quick rush of sympathy at beholding them, while the faces of king and courtier alike wore a look 'twixt smiles and tears. I doubt not that this forgetting act of my lady's recalled a like moment of joy to each; of that joy which is well-nigh pain in its intensity.

The silence at length became so heavy as to penetrate my lady's consciousness, and with a little startled cry she raised herself and stood apart from Godfrey; going red and white by turns, and seeming desirous to run away and hide like a shamed child; 'til the king, seeing this, held forth his hand with smiling grace.

"What penalty hast thou for the villain who hath done thy lover so despitefully?" questioned he.

At which Joscelyn went red and white again by turns, stammering, nor knowing what to answer. On a sudden I beheld a look of winsome mischief o'erspread her face, and quick as thought she passed to his Majesty's side, pressing a swift, fleeting kiss on his cheek.

"I know not, my liege, unless it be this," quoth she, with sweet audacity. And, by all the saints, his Majesty seemed not in the least to mislike her bold act.

Thus come I to the end of my tale, for it needs not that I say more of how in after days my lady's spirit came back again to the lightsomeness of her girlhood under a love so tender and boundless that it did compass the universe for her. And here must I pause, for I must needs lay by my penner and inkhorn and turn myself from a reverent Christian priest into Saladin and all the infidel host, and must permit myself to be charged upon, routed and beheaded with much brave and lusty shouting of, "A Bersac, a Bersac to the rescue;" all this to please a little knight who hath brown hair and eyes like speedwell flowers new opened, who fights valiantly with a baselard of wood, and a tiny shield which bears a like device with the great one that hangs on a perch in my lady's chamber: three lions and the motto, "Je suis le Roi."

And it doth seem to me not ill befitting that I bring these chronicles to a close in the words which Godfrey hath used an he finish telling his little son the story of how the motto and device was won, — a tale which the boy will be for having again and yet again.

"I would that you bear in mind, Ronald, that this motto is thy motto also, and some day thou shalt come to wear it on thy shield. Live answerably. There comes not to all the occasion of heroic deed, but to each, daily life doth bring enough of opportunity wherein to rule ourselves. So keep thy hand and heart that ere thou dost command another thou canst control thyself. Be ever ready to say with truth, 'I am the king,' over that fair but most unruly province — thine own self."

THE END

Historical Romances.

THE KING'S HENCHMAN. A Chronicle of the Sixteenth Century. Brought to light and edited by WILLIAM HENRY JOHNSON. 12mo. Cloth, extra, gilt top, $1.50.

A story of pure love and stirring action. It purports to be told by an inseparable attendant of Henry of Navarre, and that hero of a hundred fights and as many gallant adventures is made to live again for us.

> We close the book reluctantly. The hours spent in reading "The King's Henchman" were richly rewarded. — *Atlanta Constitution*.
>
> What is more noticeable than the interest of the story itself is Mr. Johnson's intuitive insight and thorough understanding of the period. While the book is Weyman in vigorous activity, it is Dumas in its brilliant touches of romanticism. — *Boston Herald*.
>
> Mr. Johnson has caught the spirit of the period, and has painted in Henry of Navarre a truthful and memorable historical portrait. — *The Mail and Express*, New York.

THE COUNT'S SNUFF-BOX. A Romance of Washington and Buzzard's Bay in the War of 1812. By GEORGE R. R. RIVERS, author of "The Governor's Garden," "Captain Shays, a Populist of 1786," etc. Illustrated by Clyde O. DeLand. 12mo. Cloth, gilt top, $1.50.

The story of "The Count's Snuff-Box" is founded on an incident of the War of 1812. In January of that year an adventurer, calling himself Count de Crillon, appeared in Washington, and for some weeks was the central social attraction of the capital. He bore letters from prominent members of Napoleon's government to M. Serurier, then Minister from France. His motive was ostensibly to help France, and injure Great Britain and the Federalists, but his real object was to secure money for John Henry's letters. In this he finally succeeded, the United States government purchasing them for fifty thousand dollars.

CAPTAIN SHAYS. A Populist of 1786. By GEORGE R. R. RIVERS, author of "The Count's Snuff-Box." 16mo. Cloth, extra, gilt top, $1.25.

THE GOVERNOR'S GARDEN. A Relation of some Passages in the Life of His Excellency, Thomas Hutchinson, sometime Captain-General and Governor-in-Chief of His Majesty's Province of Massachusetts Bay. By GEORGE R. R. RIVERS. With frontispiece. 12mo. Cloth, $1.50.

IN BUFF AND BLUE. Being Certain Portions from the Diary of Richard Hilton, Gentleman of Haslet's Regiment of Delaware Foot, in our Ever Glorious War of Independence. By GEORGE BRYDGES RODNEY. 16mo. Cloth, extra, gilt top, $1.25.

HASSAN, A FELLAH. A Romance of Palestine. By HENRY GILLMAN. Crown 8vo. Cloth, $2.00.

The author of this powerful romance lived in Palestine for over five years, and during his residence there had unusual and peculiar advantages for seeing and knowing the people and the country. He has selected the present time for the story, but has drawn freely from all the rich treasures of the past for ornament. The portions connected with the "Thar," or blood-feud between the Syrian villages, and the insurrection in Crete are not only of uncommon interest and power, but are also intensely dramatic.

> A biblical, patriarchal, pastoral spirit pervades it. Indeed, the whole book is saturated with the author's reverence for the Holy Land, its legends, traditions, glory, misery, — its romance, in a word, and its one supreme glory, the impress of the Chosen of God and of the Master who walked among them. — *The Independent.*
>
> Mr. Gillman has certainly opened up a new field of fiction. The book is a marvel of power, acute insight, and clever manipulation of thoroughly grounded truths. The story is as much of a giant in fiction as its hero is among men. — *Boston Herald.*
>
> The book is one that seems destined to take hold of the popular heart as strongly as did "Ben Hur" or "Quo Vadis," nor is it less worthy of such popularity than either of those named. — *Art Interchange.*
>
> It is romance of the strongest type. Many pages fairly glow with color, as the author in his enthusiasm portrays the natural beauties of the Holy Land. — *Public Opinion.*
>
> The hero of "Hassan, a Fellah," will be a revelation even to those who carry their ethnological studies beyond the realm of fiction. — *N. Y. Times.*

"**QUO VADIS.**" A Narrative of the Time of Nero. By HENRYK SIENKIEWICZ. Translated from the Polish by Jeremiah Curtin. Library Edition. With map and photogravure plates. Crown 8vo. Cloth, $2.00.

Popular Edition. 12mo. Cloth, 75 cents.

Of intense interest to the whole Christian civilization.—Chicago Tribune.

With him we view, appalled, Rome, grand and awful, in her last throes. The picture of the giant Ursus struggling with the wild animal is one that will always hold place with such literary triumphs as that of the chariot race in "Ben Hur." — *Boston Courier.*

Mr. Curtin's English is so limpid and fluent that one finds it difficult to realize that he is reading a translation. — *Philadelphia Church Standard.*

"**QUO VADIS.**" ILLUSTRATED HOLIDAY EDITION. With maps and plans of Ancient Rome, and twenty-seven photogravure plates from pictures by Howard Pyle, Edmund H. Garrett, E. Van Muyden, and other artists. 2 vols. 8vo. Cloth, extra, gilt top, in box, $6.00.

Half crushed Levant morocco, extra, gilt top, $12.00.

WITH FIRE AND SWORD. An Historical Novel of Poland and Russia. By HENRYK SIENKIEWICZ. Translated from the Polish by Jeremiah Curtin. With portrait of the author, plates, and map. Library Editions. Crown 8vo. Cloth, $2.00.

Popular Edition. 12mo. Cloth. $1.00.

The only modern romance with which it can be compared for fire, sprightliness, rapidity of action, swift changes, and absorbing interest is "The Three Musketeers" of Dumas. — New York Tribune.

"With Fire and Sword" is the first of a trilogy of historical romances of Poland, Russia, and Sweden. Their publication has been received throughout the United States by readers and critics as an event in literature. Action in the field has never before been described in any language so briefly, so vividly, and with such a marvellous expression of energy. The famous character of Zagloba has been described as "a curious and fascinating combination of Falstaff and Ulysses." Charles Dudley Warner, in "Harper's Magazine," affirms that the Polish author has in Zagloba *given a new creation to literature.*

THE DELUGE. An Historical Novel of Poland, Sweden, and Russia. By HENRYK SIENKIEWICZ. Translated from the Polish by Jeremiah Curtin. A sequel to "With Fire and Sword." With a map of the country at the period in which the events of "The Deluge" and "With Fire and Sword" take place. Library Edition. 2 vols. Crown 8vo. Cloth, $3.00.

Popular Edition. 2 vols. 12mo. Cloth, $1.50.

It even surpasses in interest and power the same author's romance, "With Fire and Sword." . . . *The whole story swarms with brilliant pictures of war, and with personal episodes of battle and adventure.* — New York Tribune.

Marvellous in its grand descriptions. — *Chicago Inter-Ocean.*

One of the direct anointed line of the kings of story-telling. — *Literary World.*

A really great novelist. . . . To match this story one must turn to the masterpieces of Scott and Dumas. — *Philadelphia Press.*

PAN MICHAEL. An Historical Novel of Poland, Russia, and the Ukraine. By HENRYK SIENKIEWICZ. Translated from the Polish by Jeremiah Curtin. A sequel to "With Fire and Sword" and "The Deluge." Library Edition. Crown 8vo. Cloth, $2.00.

Popular Edition. 12mo. Cloth, 75 cents.

This work completes the great Polish trilogy. The period of the story is 1668–1674, and the principal historical event is the Turkish invasion of 1672. Pan Michael, a favorite character in the preceding stories, and the incomparable Zagloba figure throughout the novel. The most important historical character introduced is Sobieski, who was elected king in 1674.

No word less than "Excelsior" will justly describe the achievement of the trilogy of novels of which "Pan Michael" is the last. — Baltimore American.

There is no falling off in interest in this third and last book of the series; again Sienkiewicz looms as one of the great novel writers of the world. — *The Nation.*

From the artistic standpoint, to have created the character of Zagloba was a feat comparable with Shakespeare's creation of Falstaff and Goethe's creation of Mephistopheles. — *The Dial.*

HISTORICAL ROMANCES. 5

ANDRONIKE. The Heroine of the Greek Revolution. Translated from the Greek of STEPHANOS THEODOSUS XENOS by Edwin A. Grosvenor, Professor of European History in Amherst College, and author of "Constantinople." 12mo. Cloth, $1.50.

Modern Greece may be proud of having given the world an historical romance like this. Viewed merely as a story, it is a work of absorbing interest in its plot and execution. At the same time, no other book, whether description, travels, or pure romance, offers so faithful and complete a picture of Greek life to-day. The reader follows the vicissitudes of hero and heroine with rapt attention, and all the time seems breathing Greek air under a Greek sky and living among the Greeks.

A book well worth reading, because it is a story of thrilling interest and it presents the best description of a memorable conflict for national liberty. — *Detroit Tribune.*

A book which is drama and action from one end to the other. Altogether a most fascinating work. — *New York Home Journal.*

I AM THE KING. Being the Account of some Happenings in the Life of Godfrey de Bersac, Crusader Knight. By SHEPPARD STEVENS. 16mo. Cloth, $1.25.

This is a romantic story of the days of Saladin and Richard Cœur de Leon. Its author has wrought into it much of the color of the home-life of the period and many of the quaint superstitions and folk-lore. The scene of the story is in part laid in England and in part in the Holy Land.

THE HEAD OF A HUNDRED. Being an Account of Certain Passages in the Life of Humphrey Huntoon, Esq., sometyme an Officer in the Colony of Virginia. Edited by MAUD WILDER GOODWIN, author of "The Colonial Cavalier." 16mo. Cloth, extra, gilt top, $1.25.

It is as sweet and pure a piece of fiction as we have read for many a day, breathing, as it does, the same noble air, the lofty tone, and the wholesome sentiment of "Lorna Doone." — *The Bookman.*

WHITE APRONS. A Romance of Bacon's Rebellion, Virginia, 1676. By MAUD WILDER GOODWIN. 16mo. Cloth, extra, gilt top, $1.25.

A beautiful little story, sweet and inspiring, not less clever than true. — *New York Times.*

A charming story. . . . Its fidelity to the conditions prevailing in the Virginia colony at the time is carefully sustained. — *The Review of Reviews.*

A WOMAN OF SHAWMUT. A Romance of Colonial Times. Boston, 1640. By EDMUND JANES CARPENTER. With twelve charming full-page illustrations and numerous chapter headings from pen-and-ink drawings by F. T. Merrill. 16mo. Cloth, extra, gilt top, with cameo design, $1.25.

CINQ-MARS; or, A Conspiracy under Louis XIII. By Count ALFRED DE VIGNY. Translated by William Hazlitt. With thirteen exquisite full-page etchings by Gaujean from designs by A. Dawant, and numerous smaller illustrations (head and tail pieces) in the text. 2 vols. 8vo. Cloth, gilt top, $6.00.

It is one of the masterpieces of French romantic fiction, . . . and a book to be always read and remembered. — *New York Mail and Express.*

THE PRINCESS OF CLÈVES. An Historical Romance of the Court of Henry II. By MADAME DE LA FAYETTE. With preface by Anatole France. Translated by Thomas Sergeant Perry. Most exquisitely illustrated with four full-page etchings and eight etched vignettes by Jules Garnier, also a portrait of the author engraved by Lamotte. The letterpress choicely printed on handmade paper at the University Press, Cambridge. 2 vols. 16mo. Cloth, extra, gilt top, $3.75.

Madame de la Fayette was the first to introduce naturalness into fiction, — the first to draw human beings and real feelings; and thereby she earned a place among the true classics. — *Preface by Anatole France.*

HISTORICAL ROMANCES. 7

THE MASTER MOSAIC WORKERS (*Les Maîtres Mosaïstes*). Translated from the French of GEORGE SAND by Charlotte C. Johnston. With a portrait of Titian, etched by W. H. W. Bicknell. 16mo. Cloth, extra, gilt top, $1.25.

A story of Venice in the time of Titian and Tintoretto, who figure prominently in the work. The mosaic work executed in the restoration of the basilica of St. Mark is fully described, and George Sand has followed very closely the facts as given by Vasari regarding the brothers Zuccati and Bartolomeo Bozza. The story is one of exquisite beauty and great power.

"The Master Mosaic Workers" is *one of the most delightful of historical novels*, and gives a vivid picture of the life in Venice at the time when Titian, Tintoretto, and Giorgione were in their zenith, and when the famous mosaics which still adorn St. Mark's were being made. — *Literary World*.

THE PRINCE OF THE HOUSE OF DAVID; or, Three Years in the Holy City. Being a Series of Letters of Adina, a Jewess of Alexandria, supposed to be sojourning in Jerusalem in the days of Herod, addressed to her father, a wealthy Jew in Egypt, and relating, as if by an eye-witness, all the scenes and wonderful incidents in the life of Jesus of Nazareth, from his Baptism in Jordan to his Crucifixion on Calvary. By Rev. J. H. INGRAHAM. 12mo. Cloth, $1.00.

New Illustrated Edition. With twenty-six engravings by Victor A. Searles. 12mo. $2.00.

Popular Edition. 16mo. Cloth, 50 cents.

These editions contain the author's latest revisions, he having availed himself of hints and suggestions contained in numerous private letters from eminent and learned men of various denominations, who have pointed out errors and suggested alterations and improvements.

THE PILLAR OF FIRE; or, Israel in Bondage. Being an Account of the Wonderful Scenes in the Life of the Son of Pharaoh's Daughter (Moses), together with Picturesque Sketches of the Hebrews under their Taskmasters. By Rev. J. H. INGRAHAM. 12mo. Cloth, $1.00.

New Illustrated Edition. With twenty-one engravings by Victor A. Searles. 12mo. $2.00.

THE THRONE OF DAVID, from the Consecration of the Shepherd of Bethlehem to the Rebellion of Prince Absalom. Being an Illustration of the Splendor, Power, and Dominion of the Reign of the Shepherd, Poet, Warrior, King, and Prophet, Ancestor and Type of Jesus; in a Series of Letters addressed by an Assyrian Ambassador to his Lord and King on the Throne of Nineveh. By Rev. J. H. INGRAHAM. 12mo. Cloth, $1.00.

New Illustrated Edition. With twenty-one engravings by Victor A. Searles. 12mo. $2.00.

BULWER'S HISTORICAL ROMANCES.
Comprising: —
  Devereux. 2 vols.
  The Last Days of Pompeii. 1 vol.
  Rienzi, the Last of the Roman Tribunes. 2 vols.
  The Last of the Barons. 2 vols.
  Leila and Calderon, Pausanias the Spartan. 1 vol.
  Harold, the Last of the Saxon Kings. 2 vols.

12mo. With frontispiece by Edmund H. Garrett. Per volume, plain cloth, $1.25; decorated cloth, gilt top, $1.50.

Any story can be supplied separately.

The new library edition of Bulwer's works is one of exceeding beauty, the size, type, paper, and binding of the volumes making them "a delight to the eye and to the touch." — *The Watchman.*

www.ingramcontent.com/pod-product-compliance
Lightning Source LLC
Chambersburg PA
CBHW021834230426
43669CB00008B/968